MOVING THE GOALPOSTS

MOVING THE GOALPOSTS

Football's Exploitation

ED HORTON

MAINSTREAM
PUBLISHING

EDINBURGH AND LONDON

First published in Great Britain in 1997 by
MAINSTREAM PUBLISHING COMPANY (EDINBURGH) LTD
7 Albany Street
Edinburgh EH1 3UG

ISBN 1 85158 863 9

A catalogue record for this book is available from the British Library

Typeset in Plantin
Printed and bound in Great Britain by Butler and Tanner Ltd, Frome

For Ruth, who would have understood

CONTENTS

EXCUSES AND ACKNOWLEDGEMENTS

To get the Oscar-ceremony bit over with first, thanks to everyone who helped and encouraged me in the writing of this book. Thanks to Dave Bowler and Harry Ritchie for advice. Thanks to the many supporters who helped out, especially Tony from Stevenage, Gary from Lincoln, Paul and Jules from Crewe, John, Ian and Paul from Brighton, and any number of others whom I may have forgotten. This book has changed a lot in the writing and much of the material they helped me with has not been used. All the more reason to thank them for their help. Many thanks, also, to Ann Reynolds, my agent, who I wish well in her retirement (which I trust that I did not induce) and to everyone at Mainstream.

Chris Fyfe has considerably added to my knowledge of Scottish football, and all the Oxford fanzine people have helped me develop my ideas about the game. Much of what I know I owe to numerous contributors to the magazines *When Saturday Comes* and *The Absolute Game*. My thanks to Andy Lyons and to Archie MacGregor for allowing me to use material from those magazines. I have also ripped off my own articles shamelessly, my 18th chapter especially, which bears a considerable similarity to an article I wrote for *WSC* on the same subject.

Among the publications from which I have borrowed material for this book, I can recall the *Daily Telegraph*, the *Financial Times*, the *Guardian*, the *Investors' Chronicle*, *Labour Research*, *Private Eye*, *Scotland on Sunday*, and, again, the indispensable *TAG* and *WSC*. I have also used handouts from the Football Supporters' Association and Football Fans Against The Criminal Justice Act.

9

This book might well be possible without Annette, but pretty much everything else would be unthinkable.

Nomenclature. I have referred throughout to Sky TV rather than BSkyB or whatever. I have happily used the terms *Premiership* and *the Premier League* almost interchangeably. If they can't make up their minds what to call themselves, I don't see why I should try to keep up. I have found myself using the term *football* in many different senses, meaning many different things – the football authorities, the supporters, the spirit of the game, or whatever. Readers will, I'm sure, understand in each case what I mean.

This book focuses on the class and economic aspects of the game, somewhat to the exclusion of other issues. My apologies if this appears to narrow my perspective. I am aware that if I write that football used to welcome everybody to the ground, that was far more likely to be true if you were white, and male, rather than black, female, or both. I have used terms like *chairman* and *businessman* because football is currently so male-dominated as to make any qualification essentially redundant. Many other books remain to be written about football's horrendous and continuing history of discrimination.

This is a book of opinions. I have been a football supporter for 15 years, and I have tried, from that perspective, to understand what has gone wrong with football, and why. I have tended to assume a working knowledge of recent developments and prominent individuals in football. Most of this book was written between March and June 1997, and some of its information will inevitably be out of date. No doubt I will have made mistakes of fact as well as errors of analysis. I trust that readers will not to be loth to put me right where they know better!

This is not an optimistic book. I do not see much cause for optimism. Since *Fever Pitch*, football has usually been written about with humour and with an emphasis on the positive. I am sorry if my vision is a rather darker one. Perhaps one anecdote to lighten the mood a little. In the course of writing this book, I went to London to watch Leyton Orient play Merthyr in the FA Cup. I got off the Tube and walked round to the pub. Having enjoyed a few drinks and read the sports pages, I picked up my paper at a quarter past two to make my way to Brisbane Road, and happened to notice that the fixture list did not appear to mention the FA Cup. I further noticed that Leyton Orient seemed to be playing in the Third Division, and away from home. I thought about checking it with the locals, until the thought of the resulting public embarrassment stopped me. Besides, the paper was quite right. It was a wasted journey. I had got completely the wrong Saturday.

Ed Horton, August 1997

In societies where modern conditions of production prevail, all life presents itself as an immense accumulation of spectacles.

Guy Debord

1. THE CRISIS AND THE BOOM

Football has sold its soul, and we are paying the price.

It has found out how to make a lot of money, but it has forgotten the supporters who sustain it. Its new-found wealth has made the fortunes of a lucky few, but it has done nothing to secure the future of the game. That future is less certain than it ever was before. Football, for its popularity, for all the money it is making, is in a state of terminal division. The game has fallen into crisis.

The profits are very great, but they are so unequally distributed that they serve only to destabilise the game. They wreck its equilibrium. They have been cornered by a very few clubs who sit at the apex of the game. That bloated segment of the Premiership has become an avaricious and expensive circus, aloof from the supporters, and for many of them, so unaffordable that it is permanently out of reach. Meanwhile the rest of the game, left behind in the gold rush, fears for its survival. The game is split between the rich clubs and the poor, and divided again, between those who benefit from the commercial revolution, and the supporters, who are paying for it.

It was not supposed to be like this. This should have been a golden age, a perfect time to be a football supporter. Heysel and Hillsborough were in the past. We had seen off most of the hooligans and nearly all the fences. Where we were once the enemy within, we were now the height of fashion. Advertisers competed for our custom. Instead of being thrown out of pubs for wearing football scarves, we were made welcome. Newspapers ceased to use the word *supporter* as a synonym for *hooligan*. They even credited us with intelligence and began to seek out our

13

opinions. TV programmes, plays and even opera took an interest in our lives. *Fever Pitch* came out. Football shirts were everywhere.

There was a boom. Everybody wanted to watch football on the television. Everybody wanted to discuss it on the television. This should have been everything we ever wanted. Instead, just when it was, at last, all right to be a football fan, everything went sour. Football solved some of its old problems, but only by creating new ones that were even more urgent, and even more damaging to its fans.

Football fans were fêted in the media, only to find themselves thrown off their own territory, struggling to find the money it costs to watch the game. Ticket prices doubled. Then they trebled. Elsewhere, many fans considered themselves lucky if they still had a team to watch. Football clubs began to run up enormous debts. The possibility of ever paying them off receded to infinity. Administrators and receivers became even more familiar with football clubs than they were before.

There has been a boom in football, but it has been a boom that has benefited just a few. A boom for the few becomes a crisis for the many. When football discovered that it had a new and untapped audience for tickets, television and merchandise, it was set free – free from its own supporters. When clubs discovered that demand for tickets exceeded supply, when they realised they could price their fans out of the market and still attract a larger crowd than they had done for years, then our place was no longer secure within the very game, the only game, we thought was ours. And when we did get in, we didn't count for much. The income from television threatened to overtake the income from the turnstiles, making the paying supporter irrelevant, shifted round the clock according to the whim of satellite TV, no more than a backdrop to the view of a much less committed, but far larger, audience on television.

The money that television audience has generated has been all but monopolised by the biggest and most profitable clubs. Once the Premiership began in 1992, the rest of football found itself fighting against insuperable odds. Yet every further development in football has made the financial predicament even worse. When the Bosman judgement threatened to cut off the revenue from player sales, a source of revenue which kept most clubs alive, the gap between big clubs and smaller ones, which had already grown into a chasm, threatened to become the difference between existence and extinction.

Yet while this crisis grows, almost nothing is done to avert catastrophe. The usual response is to try and think of ways to make it worse. The more it is made harder for most clubs to survive, the more they're told that they are living a privileged existence, dependent on subsidies that they don't deserve. In Scotland, part-time clubs are rebuked by David Murray, and Fergus McCann, for bringing down the likes of Rangers and Celtic. The rules are simple. If something benefits the poorer clubs, it's *subsidy*. But rearrange football in the interests of the richest, and it's *business*.

In England, the League Cup is encouraged to slowly die because it doesn't suit the European qualifiers, and never mind what suits the smaller clubs with their need for income from the cups. The TV deal for the Football League, and its voting rights, is renegotiated, with ever larger slices of money and power being awarded to the top division. The lower half of the Premiership, thinking it had the best of the bargain when the TV money was handed out, now quakes at the threat of pay-per-view and individual TV deals, which will cream off into a few clubs' hands most of the money that the rest of the Premiership currently receives. Whatever the rich require, they shall have. European Leagues are proposed to meet the requirements of the major clubs. But for the rest of football, there is next to nothing.

Years ago, we used to criticise the FA and the League for failing to act in the best interests of the game. Now, there is no 'game'. Clubs are businesses, and only that, and if they are not permitted to act entirely in their interests, or if the authorities incur their displeasure, they threaten to go squealing to the courts. Decisions affecting the game are now more likely to be made by a judge than anyone at the Premier League or at Lancaster Gate. The brute power of money, and the selfish ethics that go with it, have prevailed. Football is worse than split, more than divided. It has splintered. In place of its history and its traditions, it has I'm-all-right-Jack and every-man-for-himself.

Football is money. The football pages are a blizzard of figures, an ever-increasing row of noughts. You cannot get away from it. If it is not share prices, it is television revenue. If it is not television revenue, it is ever higher salaries. I was following football for many years before I knew or cared about the monetary value of a Cup win, or a League title, let alone the salaries of players, or the price of television coverage. I knew the colours of the shirts of different clubs, the names of their grounds, their honours and their nicknames. Now every fan who reads, and thinks about the game, is obliged to accumulate all sorts of information that we would rather be without.

We need to know about the implications of the Bosman judgement and the rules relating to players out of contract. We need to know about the regulations involving the use of players from outside the European Union and inside it. We have to keep abreast of decisions in the Dutch courts relating to the sale of television rights for football games, and we have to be aware of the attitude of the Office of Free Trading towards the same issue here, and the likely implications of that attitude for the future of the Premiership. We have to follow movements on the stock market as well as changing League positions. We need to know about our club's financial situation, to learn to read company accounts, and to understand both what they tell us, and what they obscure. We are only football supporters. We come to football matches to get away from this sort of thing. Yet we find ourselves acting as journalists, accountants and economists, all because money has become more important than the football which creates it.

What is football *for*? Supporters do not judge their club by the profit that it makes. Our season doesn't stand or fall by whatever figure appears on the bottom line in the accounts. Our enjoyment of a game is not proportionate to the income from the television rights. Money is merely a means to an end, a way to keep the club alive and to buy new players. When we say our clubs *succeed*, that may mean anything from avoiding relegation to winning the European Cup, but it is a football question and we give a football answer. Yet now the thing is stood upon its head. Success is merely a means of generating cash.

Money has always played a prominent part in football. But there is a world of difference between, on the one hand, recognising that you have to live in the real world, making sure you can survive within that world, and on the other, deciding that the rules and values of the market shall prevail in their entirety. In the first case, you try and cater for everyone as best you can. In the second, you ask for nothing, cater for nobody, and think of nothing but the money to be made. That is the kind of football that we have today. If it seems to many supporters that, for all its popularity, football is becoming less enjoyable a place for them to be, then that is the reason. That is why we find ourselves at loggerheads with the game we love.

Football has become a mere commodity. Its only concern is how often and how expensively it can be sold, and the élite clubs, clubs which can sell themselves in as many different ways as possible, now have football to themselves. All the coaching genius in the world cannot make up the gap between the clubs who can afford to buy whatever players that they want, and the clubs who can't. Rich clubs may fail for a while, poorer clubs succeed. But the difference is becoming permanent and is getting bigger all the time. The most divisive and depressing of all the consequences of the boom has been the emergence of a few élite clubs, a charmed circle whose spending power so far outstrips the rest as to make competition meaningless.

These clubs are more brand names than they are football clubs. They sell most of the shirts by far, attract the biggest sponsors by far and attract by far the biggest viewing figures when they are, as they always are, on television. These are the clubs through which the language of marketing pervades the speech of football. They have the biggest *fanbase*, the highest *recognition factor*.

These are the clubs who have done by far the best out of the stock market flotations, flotations which have been a major factor in stretching their financial advantage to such a distance. These are the clubs who can shop for superstars, who expect, as a matter of course, to monopolise the European places, who are greedy for pay-per-view TV. The charmed circle becomes a vicious circle, as the wealth they have acquired enables them to buy themselves renewed success, which attracts even more support and sponsorship, which leaves them even further ahead than they were before.

This is probably very exciting if you are sharing in the proceeds of the new élite. For the owners and major shareholders of these clubs, the only thing more bountiful than the present is the promised munificence of the future. But for the rest of us, football is becoming predictable and tedious. Tedious, and arrogant, and alienating for supporters.

There always was a gap between the biggest of the metropolitan clubs, and the provincial teams who aspired to beat them. But at least they could aspire. No one seriously believes that clubs like Southampton, Watford or QPR have any chance of challenging for the title that all of them relatively recently threatened to win: let alone actually winning it, as Derby, Nottingham Forest and Ipswich did. The battle for the Championship was an unequal struggle, but it was a real struggle nonetheless. It has taken a real effort to make the Championship as predictable as those in Portugal, Scotland, Greece or Holland, but, for a few, it has certainly been worth it.

It has not been worth it for supporters. For the great majority who support clubs other than the élite, it is obvious that a future of restricted horizons and imperilled existence is not a vision of football that serves our interests. We have escaped the benefits of the boom, without avoiding its financial consequences. Other clubs may not be able to compete with the élite, but they still have to compete for players. Therefore their costs, and in consequence their ticket prices, have shot up for everybody. Most fans are therefore paying rather more and getting rather less.

But even those supporters who follow the élite have plenty of reasons to be sceptical about the boom. Their ticket prices are the highest, and their grounds are becoming less and less accessible to anyone who cannot find the money for a season ticket. In return, they have success. But most of them were used to that already, used to following clubs which won trophies and played European football. These fans, too, are victims of the boom. Their clubs are ever more distant from them, ever more impersonal and alienating. The bigger the club, the smaller the feeling of supporters that they still belong.

Football clubs owe their support to the idea, to the belief, that they are driven by a common purpose, that they form a community in which the players, supporters and directors work together and pull in the same direction. Never has this been less true than it is today, and nowhere is it more false than at the new élite. These clubs have nothing in common with the people who support them. The players at these clubs are paid the average annual salary once a fortnight and find it intolerable that they do not receive it once a week. The owners of these clubs possess shareholdings whose values can be measured in the tens of millions. These people do not know our names. They do not live where we do, do not live like we do, and do not think about the game like we do. Between us and them there is no community. And football is embittered by the conflict that results.

Football as we would like it, and football as it has become, are constantly in strife. The requirements of supporters and the demands of the clubs produce a disharmonious background to contemporary football. We never wanted that to happen, and we do not like it. But at least it has made us more aware. There can be few fans left who do not know that there are bitter arguments in progress about the future of the game, few who have never read a fanzine, even fewer who have not heard the things those fanzines say.

The fruits of crisis and division are discontent and protest. Fans may be fashionable, but that has not made us any more content. It has given us no reason why we should be. If anyone still thinks that football is going in the right direction, let them ask why there have been more protests by supporters in the last decade than in all the hundred years of football that preceded it.

The anger and frustration of the fans spills over everywhere. Fanzines have multiplied. The capacity for organisation that fanzines brought to light has played a growing role in football. Protests are organised, banners raised, petitions signed, red cards waved. And there have been occasional victories as a result. Bond schemes have been revised, chairmen chased out of clubs, mergers abandoned. The unaccountable have occasionally been forced to account for themselves. The press have learned to listen, and the views of supporters are regularly heard. The existence of supporters' protests and organisations, and the very fact that our interests are not the same as those of chairmen and directors, has become accepted by the public, and understood.

The supporters are the heart of football. We pay to keep it in existence, but we do far more for it than that. We are its advocates, its popularisers, its critics and crusaders. Now we are its future too. Football depends on us. The sort of football it is going to become depends on what supporters have to say about it, how vocal we are in its defence, and how much we are able to stand up for our interests. Because it is a mutual bargain. What benefits supporters, benefits football. The more football is obliged to cater for the wishes of its supporters, the better – because the closer to supporters football will become. But at the moment it is further from supporters than it has ever been.

Football has sold its soul. But we have not sold ours. Those who run the game would like us to pay up without complaint, to accept whatever we are given, to turn ourselves into the sort of spectators that they dream about. Casual, cheerful, shallow, polite and passive. Spectators, not supporters. We do not fit that mould. We do not because we care about this game. There may always be much about it that we do not like, but it is worth saving all the same. We need to try and save it. After all, it is supposed to be *our* game.

2. LIKE IT OR LUMP IT

What good to us is football that we can't afford to watch? What good to us are football clubs who charge outrageous prices for their tickets? That is the situation which confronts us now, and has done ever since clubs began to put their prices up to levels which would put a ticket tout to shame. Nothing demonstrates better what has happened to the game than what has happened to those prices. Nothing demonstrates better what football thinks of its supporters. The message is that we are here to be ripped off. That we are no more to football than a licence to print money.

The rising prices are a miracle of progress for people who make money out of football. For us, they are an unequivocal disaster. The prices charged at most of the biggest clubs – and some of the smaller ones as well – are more than many can afford. They are forcing long-term supporters out of football. For many others it has become a struggle to hang on, to find ten pounds a week out of your wages for a season ticket, to find much more to give your kids the chance to go. The Premiership can put out all the figures that it likes for rising profits and attendances. The reality for millions of supporters is a struggle to afford a ticket. When football makes its profits at the expense of fans who can't afford to go, those fans can no more be expected to applaud than a worker made redundant can be expected to wish well their former company. The sacrifices are all on the one side, the profits on the other.

Excessive ticket prices are changing football for the worse. They change the game of football into something it was never meant to be. It is not a case of buying a slightly better product for a slightly better price.

Football is becoming a different sort of game entirely. Because the very point about the game, right from the start over one hundred years ago, was that association football was a game that we could all afford to watch. Football was cheap because it was the game of those who had no cash to spare.

You didn't have to save to watch the game. Even if you were going to watch the best teams in the country, you didn't have to make arrangements months before the game. To watch a match you didn't even have to ask about the price of tickets in advance. You knew you could afford to go. You knew your friends could go. Football was there for everyone who wanted it. It was our game. It was accessible. It was attainable. Now much of football is becoming unattainable, exclusive, and is proud of it.

Football is moving out of reach. The racheting of prices is a brutal process, and a cynical one, but one, already, to which we are accustomed. No one expects to find it easy to afford a ticket for the top end of the Premiership. No one expects to find it easy to afford a ticket when a club has moved to a brand new and expensive ground. As for the prices if you want a ticket for a game at Wembley, only a new or part-time fan can be surprised at the extortionate amounts they have to pay.

It doesn't even have to be an international, or a game between the glamour clubs. When Swansea City played Northampton Town in the Third Division play-off final, the cheapest tickets cost no less than £15. And those were tickets for the lousy seats. A decent view would have cost you £28. Yet those prices are relatively cheap. Cup semi-finals cost supporters twice as much. When football fans were all accused of being hooligans, we were supposed to be ashamed of going to a football match. Now it has become an achievement to be proud of, if we can actually afford to buy a ticket for a game between two leading clubs.

We are already used to it. We take it for granted. Yet it has only been that way for just a few short years. Football avoided ripping off supporters for a hundred years, and for the last decade it has been doing everything it can to make up for lost time. It's startling to realise how recently the era of cheap football still existed. I went to Anfield in 1987. The Liverpool team I saw, with Barnes, Beardsley and Aldridge, went on to win the Championship at a stroll. They were quite probably the best team in the whole of Europe. The price they charged me for a ticket was £3.

Three pounds to see the best team in the country. Allow for ten years of inflation, and in real terms, three quid in 1987 still wouldn't add up to a fiver now. But you won't get into Anfield for a fiver. You won't get into Anfield for a tenner. There's scarcely a single stadium in the Premiership where ten pounds will come even close to getting you a ticket. Five pounds won't even buy you football in the Third Division.

Liverpool and Everton were always noted for keeping prices relatively low, in deference to the economic circumstances of fans on Merseyside. Tottenham were quicker to take advantage of their supporters' generosity. They were charging them £3 as long ago as 1983. That year the price went up from £2.40 on the ingenious grounds that it would be easier for turnstile operators to give change. But even Tottenham, in 1987, charged no more than £3.50 for the cheapest tickets. The fan who goes to White Hart Lane today can say goodbye to 20 quid. Nobody bothers thinking up ingenious excuses any more. Like it or lump it, is the attitude. To Alan Sugar, this is economic sense. But if you squeeze supporters for every extra penny that they've got, you cannot then expect those fans to like it.

At nearly every top division club the same applies. The last time I enquired about a ticket to see Blackburn, the cheapest price was £15. Coventry City was the same. Southampton asked for £17. Stamford Bridge is closed to anyone with less than £20. A Chelsea ticket, back in 1987, cost £4. Buying a season ticket for Chelsea in 1997-8 would have set their supporters back at least £370, and that was not the highest in the Premiership. Anybody who wanted to watch Chelsea from the middle tier of the East Stand would have paid out nearly £900. More than £40 a match. Who can afford prices like that? If prices like that are going to become the norm, ordinary supporters are going to have no chance at all to watch their clubs.

Chelsea, at least, are better than they were in 1987. But since when did the price that we are asked to pay have any real correlation with the quality of football that we get? On being relegated, Nottingham Forest put their prices up by 25 per cent. Nor is lower division football always much cheaper than the Premiership. In 1996-97, Northampton Town charged £11. Burnley, in Division Two, charged more. Both of these clubs, and several others quite a long way down the League, charged rather more than Sheffield Wednesday, who finished just off the European places in the Premiership.

If prices have gone up it doesn't mean a better standard of football is on offer. If Fulham charge three times the price they did in 1985, while playing football at a lower level, is the rise in price connected to a better quality of football? But the problem is not restricted to a few clubs charging more than they deliver. It is a problem of *all* clubs charging more, much more, not just a few, nor even those who could plausibly claim to offer better football for their increased prices.

The rising prices are supposed to be justified by the wealth of foreign talent on display in English football. But hyperinflation has applied throughout the four professional divisions. A ticket price of £8 to get in to Craven Cottage can hardly be justified by the quality of international players in the Premiership.

Nor are Premiership clubs, even the biggest and most bloated, charging us more because they play to higher standards than their predecessors. Aston Villa do not expect to win the European Cup again any time soon, but they cost rather more to watch, in real terms, than did the European champions of 1982. The Liverpool side that finished fourth in 1997 hardly compared to any of their great teams from the Shankly or the Paisley years. What do we have to show for all the extra money they are asking from us? Very little. But the prices carry on rising, year on year, no matter whether the extortioners fail to win the Premiership, fail in Europe, or fail to produce the sort of awesome football we ought to see by right if we are paying awesome prices to see it.

Ten years ago we watched our football through a grille of metal and barbed wire. These have gone, and that at least is something to be thankful for. But as the cages should never have been erected in the first place, there is no way we should have to pay more for the privilege. It is not as if the ticket prices went down when the fences went up. The difference is not in the football, nor even the conditions in which supporters watch it. It is partly that unprecedented television coverage has brought about an increased awareness of football, and with it a rise in public interest. It is also that football became fashionable.

The social stigma has disappeared. More people than before want to watch the game. Many of them have more money to spend than the average supporter of ten years ago. Demand exceeds supply. That is why the football club can blackmail the supporter with the most exorbitant price demand that they can get away with. If you won't pay it, we can find someone who will. That is the grim reality.

That is the way the market is supposed to work. The seller charges the highest price they think they can, the buyer pays only what they are prepared to pay, or goes elsewhere. At the middle the two meet up, an equilibrium is reached, the market price established. By that logic, all prices are acceptable by virtue of the fact that the buyer, acting freely, is prepared to pay them.

That is the system under which we live. The same rules govern the price of bread, the price of beer, the price of houses. The businessmen in charge of football would be surprised to hear that football should be any different. Why should it be? They can see nothing for anybody to complain about. Why change a system which is bringing them so much success? Does not the fact that prices have gone up prove by itself that the product is much better than before?

Yet that complacency obscures the issue rather than settles it. You do not solve an argument about football by producing sets of constantly increasing figures representing income and success. If the leading Premiership clubs, or, for that matter, clubs at any level, are no better, by any objective standard, than their counterparts from 20 years ago, then higher ticket prices do not prove otherwise – any more than when a house price doubled in the Eighties, that house was twice as good as it was before the price went up. It is a nonsense and a most convenient smokescreen for rapaciousness. That is the true relationship that price rises reveal between a club and its supporters. It's not a friendly bargain struck between consenting parties. It is a case of withholding what we desperately want, and need, until we are prepared to beg for it.

It isn't hard to charge supporters more to watch something as vital to them as their football club. The starving will do anything to pay for food, the addict anything to get their fix. To those for whom the game is both nourishment and addiction, there may be no such thing as ticket prices that we cannot pay, just prices that we can't afford to pay. We know we shouldn't. We know we ought to tell them where to draw the line. People who will go without a holiday to buy a season ticket, or who will risk the sack to watch a match, are people who are ripe to be exploited. We know that. We have always known that. But until recently, that exploitation was an exception, not the rule, and that exploitation is beginning to force out even some of the addicts and the diehards.

If inflation follows inevitably from an increase in demand, why has football not ripped us off in quite this way before? When attendances reached record highs in the years after World War II, football was cheap. After the ending of the maximum wage, when George Best was at his peak and England won the 1966 World Cup, it stayed, stubbornly and resolutely, cheap. Demand was high. Attendances were not just higher than they were around the middle of the Eighties, they were much higher than they are now. Grounds were full. But supporters' wallets were not emptied.

Perhaps, however many fans there were, few could afford a higher ticket price? But gentrification is nothing new in football. When Fulham and Chelsea were trendy in the Sixties, Craven Cottage and Stamford

Bridge were no strangers to the metropolitan middle class. Yet, whatever happened to the ticket prices, there was nothing like the open insolence of clubs towards supporters we are familiar with today.

Why? Demand, supply and prices produce too complex an equation for anyone to pin the reasons down exactly. But there is a social dimension too. A question of the ethics and the motives of the people who run football clubs. Only recently has it been possible to get rich running a football club. It's not the first time anybody tried to make a living out of it, but it is the first time that rapid accumulation of a profit has been the actual purpose of the game. If, until now, they never took the chance to rip us off, perhaps nobody ever looked for it. Before the chairmen looked on football as their business, rather than their hobby, football was not conceived of as a cash-cow. And possibly, the overt greed which rules in football would not have been acceptable until the worst years of the Eighties, until the opposition to such avariciousness, in society and in politics, had been crushed.

Until the purpose of all industry, from gas to television to the running of the railways, was understood to be solely the production of the largest profit possible, then turning football into a honeypot would not have been so easy or so swift. Those greedy years are gone. Their values have been examined and rejected. But football continues to bear their shameless mark. Half-price tickets for children seem to have disappeared. Concessions for the unemployed seem to have disappeared. There is no place for social conscience in the people's game.

It is difficult to see how we are going to get cheap football back again. The exclusion of the dedicated but hard-up supporter will continue to be an offensive reality. There are those who suggest that when Newcastle, or Manchester United, or Arsenal, extend their stadia or move to larger premises, some of the fans who currently cannot afford it will be able to return. I hope so. It would be nice if all the Geordies who faithfully put up with failure at St James's Park, for all those years, were able to get in to see them now they have a team that's worthy of its fans. But that will probably not be what happens.

Higher attendances for clubs like these will only mean they dominate the country even more, enabling them to attract even larger numbers of well-off supporters, keeping the prices high, keeping the poorer fans out of the ground. These clubs will charge the most expensive prices that they can, and if Euro 96 has taught us anything, it is that football prefers expensive tickets, and a half-full ground, rather than pitch its prices at any price lower than it has to.

There is no end in sight to this extortion. But it is not even the money that matters most about it. Few of us would begrudge our clubs a few more quid if they honestly told us that they really needed it. We do not watch our teams for money. Money is not something we expect to get out of it. Financial considerations are not the only, or the most important ones.

Danny Blanchflower said that he would play internationals for nothing, if the supporters were let in for nothing too. If football clubs were not being run for corporate profit and for personal gain, if every penny went back into football, the price rises would not hurt half so much. What gets to fans is the impression that for all the loyalty and commitment shown by supporters, their football clubs consider that they owe them nothing. And worse than that, that their own clubs are laughing in their faces.

What good to us are football clubs who charge outrageous prices for their tickets? None. But what use, either, are football clubs who look upon their fans in the same way as a loan shark looks upon his clients? It sours our pleasure in the game. The more our football clubs insist on taking from us, the less we feel inclined to give. Nothing, however high the prices, can ever stop us from being football supporters. But once our football clubs decide to treat supporters as their enemies, being a football fan is never quite the same again. It is a lousy way for football to turn out. We always knew our hopes in football clubs would end in disappointment. But we did not expect that they would end in bitterness.

3. THE SILENCE OF THE FANS

If football supporters feel that they're being forced out of the game, they are right. Forced out. Deliberately and ruthlessly evicted. We are being financially excluded from the game. We are being squeezed out physically, as the corporate boxes and complimentary tickets take up an ever larger space within our grounds. But we are also being deliberately moved out. They want us out. Wherever possible (and at the most successful clubs, it is more than possible) they want to trade us in for a model of supporter who can afford to pay them even more.

Football no longer wants to be about traditional clubs and their traditional supporters. It would like to be about selling a product, about targeting an audience. That target audience will obviously come from the most affluent social classes football can attract. Most of football's following always previously originated from the working class. Football was cheap because that following could not afford it to be otherwise. Supporters of that sort are not good enough for football any more. They are no good for profits, no good for the share price.

So football hopes to move them out, and move a better class of person in. It hopes to fill its stands with freeloaders enjoying corporate hospitality. The corporate entertainment industry can outspend real supporters any time it wants. Newcastle, with ten thousand people on the waiting list for season tickets, chose to extend the number of corporate packages on offer rather than let some more supporters in the ground. Chelsea and the Football Association had a squabble, before the 1997 Cup final, over whether Chelsea were permitted to sell their allotted tickets in hospitality packages costing over £500 a head. The FA lectured Chelsea on their responsibilities, while charging even more than Chelsea for packages of their own. While this debate was going on, more than a thousand Middlesbrough season ticket holders were unable to get tickets for their club's first ever appearance in the final.

At Luton, the side the TV viewer sees, opposite the cameras, used to be the Bobbers' Stand, so-called after the shilling supporters paid for admission. These supporters, in the Thirties, raised the money to build the stand named after them. Fifty years later the stand was ripped out – and replaced with a row of executive boxes. The Bobbers' Stand is no longer there, and neither are the fans. That symbolises the way that football, on the pretence of bringing in money that will benefit supporters, has actually tried to get rid of us.

Football clubs have no interest in how many years of dedication their fans have shown. They only ask how much supporters have to spend. The better off they are, the more the clubs will try to keep them. The less they have to spend, the more the clubs will look for someone else to take their place. This is a strategy that major clubs have followed quite intentionally, with not a trace of sentiment, with no sense of regret. It is the way the Premiership has chosen to target itself, and it has no apology to make. Rick Parry's parting shot, before leaving the Premier League, was to shrug his shoulders at accusations that football was leaving working-class supporters in the cold: 'I don't think clubs will be depressed about their increasing numbers of affluent supporters.'

So if you can't afford to watch your heroes any more, who cares? The clubs have got nothing to cry about. One wonders how this attitude went down with any Liverpool supporters who have been priced out of Anfield so that their seats could go to affluent suburbanites. One wonders how it would have gone down with Bill Shankly.

The strategy is working. It has been, for Premiership clubs, if not for us, a fantastic success. The lower social classes are finding it increasingly impossible to watch the more expensive clubs. Attendances may be increasing but the proportion of the fans who come from lower-income groups is shrinking more rapidly all the time.

It is a rout. The annual Premiership survey of supporters shows how the poorer fans are being kicked out by the affluent. Fewer than ten per cent now come from social classes D and E, the lowest categories on the scale. The highest category is social class A. There are more Premiership supporters in that class than there are from D and E combined. Social class B possesses more than twice as many Premiership supporters than classes D and E together. The Cs are still the largest group. Many of these are mostly people from the working class, on relatively decent incomes. These people are still clinging on despite the price rises. But working-class supporters on lower incomes are on the way out. There must be many more people who watch the Premiership who pay income tax at the top rate, than there are supporters in receipt of benefits, or fans whose incomes would increase if there was a minimum wage.

Is that the social composition we would have found in football even as recently as, say, ten years ago? Is it the sort of crowd you'll find watching the Third Division? The Premiership are unloading at the bottom of the income scale and reloading at the top. It operates a policy of social cleansing, of making football suitable for the better-off by the simple means of removing the lower orders from the stands.

At the same time, they are removing half the passion, half the purpose from the game. They, and all the commercial enterprises who have jumped upon the commercial bandwagon, are trying to change it into a mere lifestyle accessory, something to fill your empty leisure time rather than something with which you fill yourself through your devotion and commitment. They are producing a more shallow game, a game more suited to spectators than supporters, a game in which its followers do not immerse themselves but one into which they pop in and pop out according to its fashionable status and their other lifestyle options.

Football ceases to be at the centre of its own universe. It becomes instead the launching pad for other games and leisure interests. It lends itself to spread betting on the accumulated shirt numbers of the scorers. It is the subject of an enormous number of advertisements. There are football bars opening up, there are glossy men's magazines which want to write about the game but wouldn't write about a real issue if they knew one when they saw it. These are not signs of an obsession with the game. They are a badge, a sign, a way of showing that one is interested in football as long as it is fashionable.

This wouldn't matter were it not that thousands of supporters have had their place in football taken by shallow but extremely well-paid yuppies. In that context it becomes offensive to see the game used as a plaything, to see so much money made from it by people whose genuine interest in the game is very small. But that is the audience that football wants, when it can get it. That is the audience it deliberately sought out.

Of course there is no reason why any individual should not be as deeply devoted to the game of football as another, whatever their income or their background, whatever the circumstances of their life. Football may be more and more exclusive now, but it has never been exclusive in the opposite way. Football is not about inverted snobbery and never sought to make the middle class unwelcome. Yet everybody knows that the guts of the game, its passion and its heart, lie mostly with the working-class supporters.

The lower down the social scale that you go, the more likely it is that your attachment to the game will verge upon the absolute. The better off you are, the more likely that your interest will be more casual, more detached. Starkly, the Premiership survey backs this picture up.

It asked respondents how devoted to their club they were, the scale running from 'one of the most important things in my life' to 'just one of the things I do'. It then divided them by income. Of those on less than ten thousand pounds a year, one in three (34.5 per cent) thought their football club was 'one of the most important things in my life', and only one in ten (9.9 per cent) considered it 'just one of the things I do'. But of supporters on more than thirty thousand pounds a year, only one in six (17.5 per cent) went for 'one of the most important things in my life', smaller than the proportion (18.6 per cent) who opted for 'just one of the things I do'. In between the two extremes, the same tendency is apparent. The higher the income bracket, the smaller the proportion of supporters who professed great attachment to the game.

It could be no other way. There are supporters who need the game of football and there are those who just appreciate it. The first group, almost literally, live for football. They live for Saturday. The second group are merely pleased when Saturday comes along. They look for entertainment and an enjoyable way to pass the time. But the first require something vital, something with fight and drama in which they must immerse themselves, something to which they show a manic loyalty in return.

Where can that need, that grasping for intensity, possibly derive from other than from our daily experience of life? And who will have the greatest need to generate some pride out of the common purpose of the football crowd? The people in the boxes may have their problems. The people in the most expensive seats may have their problems. But the desire, the intensity, the desperation, the feeling of entitlement to a return on your emotional commitment, these come mostly from those who take orders in life, not from those who give them. It comes from those who have to bottle up their frustrations in the week, not from those who take it out on their subordinates. It comes from those for whom shortness of money overshadows, and exacerbates, all the other problems of their lives. The less comfort and opportunity we have in life, the more we need our football.

But now, the more we need it, the less we are likely to get it. Football rejects those who are the most attached to it in order to attract the group who can take it or leave it. It thereby moves supporters from the centre of football to the periphery. It becomes the province of those who are content merely to watch.

Football is paying a price for what it's done. The price paid is a muted crowd, one that, increasingly, lacks some of the fire, the desire, the wilfulness of its predecessors. If the crowd conveys less power, if it feels less exciting than it did, then it serves those rich clubs right who wanted it that way. But those clubs neither notice, nor do they care. The damage done is not to the people at the top, but to the crowd itself, that central component of the game which makes football so fascinating.

Many observers have noticed that the crowd is getting quieter. The chanting is less frequent, less wholehearted. At some grounds, the fans have even started to demand that clubs create new 'singing areas'. The very fact that they need to ask for them speaks for itself.

All-seater stadia are among the reasons for the silence of the crowd. Certainly compulsory seating cramps the lungs, it dissipates the collective feeling of the crowd, it prevents its coalescence. The clubs who are keenest on bringing in a more genteel audience are well aware of this and like it very much. At Old Trafford supporters have been thrown out for having the temerity to stand up for a while and sing. That is Premiership football at its most arrogant. Show loyalty, and show enthusiasm, and you're out.

But it isn't just the seats that have muffled the voice of the crowd. It's many of the people sitting in them. At Wembley finals, the tannoy plays *We Are The Champions*, in case some of the fans don't understand that what they've seen is actually important, in case the mere event, the mere result, is not enough for them to get excited about. At internationals, Mexican waves are common during quiet periods. I never knew a football fan who liked Mexican waves. If fans are bored, if they don't think their team is doing what it should, they moan. They shout. They tell the players to get their fingers out. They call for substitutes, or for the sacking of the manager. But they do not start doing Mexican waves. If that's as much interest as these spectators have in football, what are they doing there in the first place? But they are there because they can afford to be, and the shouters, the complainers, those who rarely for a moment take their eyes off the field, are forced out, to make way for the casual fan, a fan with no abiding interest, with no expectations and with a low attention span.

These are the people football wants. The people that it doesn't want are the working-class supporters who for a hundred years made football possible. It is a policy which demonstrates a monstrous level of ingratitude. Where do we get the game of football from? From the working people who filled its grounds for more than a century. They are the reason football matters. It owes them everything. Without these people it could have had no cultural weight, no purpose, no vitality. There would have been no professionalism, and no Football League.

Where do clubs get their nicknames? Often from their identification with the local industries, and by extension those who worked in them and, in turn, often identified themselves with the football club. Mariners, Hatters, Blades and Cobblers, and many other nicknames speak of the history of football and place it squarely within the history of the working class.

Many clubs' grounds, by their surroundings, place their clubs on that same page of social history. Grounds like Kenilworth Road or Loftus Road or Highbury are jammed into small spaces between terraced houses. This is the history from which many football clubs, whenever they can, would like to escape. They'll keep the symbols. The nicknames will sell well on scarves and badges. But the reality is something they want nothing more to do with.

It is still different in the lower divisions, and even at most clubs in the Premiership many of the working-class supporters are still clinging on, refusing to be thrown away by clubs which they love in theory, but in practice cannot trust. All of these clubs would have ceased to exist many decades ago, if their working-class fans had shown the same disdain for their clubs as their clubs are showing them now. Nobody expects any better from football clubs. But knowing what they're like does not make their behaviour any more acceptable. Their greed and selfishness is only matched by their ingratitude.

They are no better than the landlord who pushes up the rent to get rid of the residents and bring in a better class of tenant. They are just as bad as the cost-cutting employer who downsizes staff, to make more money working fewer people harder. At least some of *their* victims get a pay-off when they leave. But there is no such compensation for the working-class supporters whom football has chosen to attempt to make redundant. They get nothing, and for all their dedication, both to club and game, they go without even a leaving present to show for all their decades of devotion.

4. RUN RAGGED BY PHILANTHROPISTS

The harder it gets for the fans, the easier it gets for the people in the boardroom. Club owners, chairmen, directors and chief executives alike. They run football for their own benefit. The more money it takes from its supporters, the more ends up in their own pockets. Yet at the same time as they use the game to benefit themselves, they have been able to portray themselves as benefactors and philanthropists, saviours of clubs and of the game in general. The greater the contribution that football makes to those who run it, the greater the contribution that those people claim they're making to the game.

They get away with it because their voices are the loudest, the most powerful, in football. They dominate the game. They dominate the coverage of the game. The combination of aggression, ego and financial clout allows them to play a role that up until recently would have been beyond them. Not very long ago, directors and chairmen, no matter what the extent of their personal fortune, were relatively obscure individuals. After the rise of the Shanklys and Busbys, men who made the manager the most important person in the club, who wrested team selection out of the directors' hands, those directors were hardly more prominent than a parish councillor, nor much more influential.

So, at any given club, long-serving supporters might know who was on the board, who ran the club, whose hand rested on the purse-strings. But they didn't really need to know. Nor would they have known whether they wanted to or not, in the way that we do now. Directors were not in the public eye. Nobody thought they should be. Outside the press, few people knew, or cared about, the identity even of the men who ran the country's leading clubs. It didn't seem to matter.

But now they dominate the scene, striding across the football pages with their promises, their self-delusion, their demands. Open the papers and what you get is Alan Sugar, David Sullivan, David Murray, Doug Ellis, Jack Hayward, Steve Gibson, Fergus McCann and Francis Lee, and if, on any day, none of these prophets can be found to lay down the law on any of the issues of the moment, there are dozens of their counterparts at smaller clubs who can be relied upon to let us have the benefit of their opinions.

They are so prominent, so influential that some seem bigger than the clubs themselves. It's not unusual to see their club names reproduced, in news report or match report, as if the owner's name had become embedded in the title. John Hall's Newcastle. Jack Walker's Blackburn. No doubt a few club owners might very well like to change the name so that *their* names were permanently incorporated, judging by the vulgar, but increasingly common practice of having stadiums and stands named after chairmen. The Doug Ellis Stand. The Derek Pavis Stand. The new Reading ground is to be named after John Madejski. Modest these men are not.

Their statements, and their actions, and their petty squabbles, are the soap opera of the sports pages. At one time, a change of chairman might have merited no more than a mention in the local paper, accompanied by an appreciation by a veteran football correspondent who had known him for many years. But now, internal struggle in the boardroom, who's in, who's out, is at the forefront of supporters' minds, in newspapers and in our conversation.

Michael Tabor and his rejection by West Ham. The struggle between Terry Venables and Alan Sugar. The fight to take control of Nottingham Forest. The squabbles between the late Matthew Harding and Ken Bates. The catalogue of planned takeovers at Old Trafford, from Robert Maxwell to Michael Knighton to Michael Grade. The battles at Home Park between Dan McAuley and his managers. These conflicts make good copy. Everybody likes a bit of turmoil and gossip. But they exert a real fascination because we understand that they're important, we understand it matters who controls our clubs, and it matters what those people do with that control.

If it were not for the determination of supporters to replace bad owners, hopefully with better ones, then we would not take quite the interest in events inside the boardroom that we do. If it were not for the discovery that we can sometimes force these people out, that we can make some of the changes that we want to make, then our fascination would be futile, would be no more than gawping at the doings of the rich and famous. But the public prominence of the new breed owes rather less to the influence of supporters than it does to their own craving for publicity. They have bought themselves a place in the spotlight and they intend to use it to its full potential.

There is no shortage of rich men who are keen to see how much attention they can attract by installing themselves at the head of a football club. Once Elton John and Robert Maxwell showed how much a successful club contributed towards your fame and reputation, the way was clear for a host of other would-be public benefactors to give football a throw.

Some of these may have had a genuine inclination to philanthropy. (Elton John, possibly, comes to mind.) Others may have shown some concern for the long-term health of the clubs in their possession, as well as the short-term publicity accruing in their favour. (Robert Maxwell does not immediately come to mind.) But once rich chairmen had got their claws into the game, then whatever their motivations, whatever the influence of any of them for good or ill, the game could never again be prised away from them. We could not manage without them. In football you either keep up or you lose. Once one club had a chairman who was prepared to spend a lot of money, once other clubs agreed to join them in the chase to spend as many millions as possible, then everybody had to have a millionaire of their own.

Now everybody wants to find a Jack Walker. He was the first man to actually buy himself the Premiership title. It was the most impressive demonstration of the crude power of money in the history of English football. One man was able to get what he wanted by spending his money without restraint until he got it. Once that happened, all the rules were changed forever. Almost every other club hankered after someone who could help them emulate Blackburn Rovers' success. The more that clubs attracted millionaires, the more they spent, the faster prices rose, and the more those clubs which did not have millions behind them were bound to fall behind.

So everybody wants a Jack Walker of their own. The problem is that some of them have got – almost – exactly what they wanted. They found that people were queuing up to have a go at spending millions. And after that, the clubs had no choice but to look for millionaires whether they wanted them or not, because they all needed another millionaire to clean up the mess the previous one had left behind. The more money they spent, the more they found themselves in debt. They started off looking for a benefactor and ended up looking for a saviour to bail out the club.

Football clubs have been pitched into a pit of debt, a pit from which only more rich chairmen can hope to rescue them. So clubs, and their supporters, spend their time hoping, and praying, and looking for a saviour. The smaller and more vulnerable the club, the deeper is the desperation, the more frantic the search. Every new rumour is reported in the press, and fans attempt to match the profile of each white-knight-to-be to the template of the conquering hero that they want. We seize on evidence that they are long-term supporters of the club, that they used to watch it from the terraces, that they have 'the best interests of the club at heart', that they are going to 'put their money into the club'.

But usually the people who emerge have nothing in common with the ideal we were looking for. Only the self-delusion born of desperation allows us to pretend they have, and it is not long before even that pretence becomes impossible to sustain. While the euphoria lasts, that is when we are at our most vulnerable. Our need to believe leaves us particularly open to publicity seekers and other elements who mean us no good whatsoever. We are too easily fooled and far too easily impressed.

It is not a dignified spectacle. Thousands of fans prostrate themselves before a new and beaming owner, hoping to touch them, cheering at their name. Fawning pieces appear in normally sceptical fanzines, appealing to the vanity of the owners, referring to them by their first names as if those owners were their friends. But how else are supporters expected to react? What hope is there, other than to put blind faith in the remote possibility that someone who has dedicated their life to making money might be genuinely willing to spend it on us? That is the grim reality of football in the age of the multi-million debt. We are all obliged to hunt for saviours. That being so, we want to find the best one we can get. When clubs are forced to carry debts worth millions of pounds, they have to find someone prepared to guarantee those debts. There are still some chairmen who actually are not rich businessmen, but they are becoming rather fewer. Few people outside the highest income brackets can aspire to run a football club. Very few have enough money to take on the debts.

The owners, of course, know very well that we think we cannot do without them. They take advantage of it to remind us at every turn precisely how grateful for their existence we should be. Most supporters, at one time or another, will have been told by or on behalf of their club chairman that without them the club would have closed down. They have invested time, money and dedication to save our club and all that we can do is complain and gripe about it.

At Oxford, Robert Maxwell and his supporters never tired of telling us that without him there would be no football club. By the time he died, when the club's debts were a couple of thousand per cent higher than the ones which he took on, there very nearly wasn't. A decade and a half after he took over at Stamford Bridge, having made himself a lot of money in that time, Ken Bates still finds it necessary to remind supporters of the state in which he found the club when he took over. Fergus McCann is much the same. None of these people is at all unusual. In their eyes, football is full of saviours, and those saviours are themselves.

They give themselves a lot more credit than they are due. None is as indispensable as they would like to think. Almost every club could have found other temporary solutions to their problems without calling in the particular individuals who are so exercised by our ingratitude. Oxford, rather than turn to Maxwell, could have staved off the bank with a single transfer sale, and then taken their time to find somebody more reliable, rather than panic and look for the nearest ambitious politician of dubious reputation to bail them out. Even when there is finally no alternative to calling in another millionaire, the choice is rarely, truly, limited to a shortlist of one.

There is no shortage of candidates to take over our football clubs, especially at a time when it looks like there might be money in it. Put crudely, there are something like eighty thousand millionaires in Britain. That averages out at nearly one thousand each for every professional football club. Not many need to be interested in football to still leave us with a range of possible alternatives. There always seems to be another saviour just around the corner.

Nor are these saviours quite as brave as they would like us to believe. They take very few real financial risks. I have never heard of any director who went bankrupt as a result of their involvement in a football club. If they are rich, they do not hazard any more than a fraction of their fortunes. Even Jack Walker's £50 million, which he pumped into Blackburn Rovers, pales into insignificance against a personal fortune in excess of £400 million.

Even if they spend a lot of money, it is not usually their own money that they spend. They spend their own money buying up the club. Sometimes for millions, but, sometimes, for very little. Oxford were sold in 1992 for ten thousand pounds. Terry Venables got Portsmouth for a pound. But when, in turn, they sell the club, they can expect to get their money back again. They spend their money making loans to their clubs. But when they leave the money is repaid. The cash they lend they can take back. The money spent in the meantime is usually the club's.

Club owners' reputation for putting money into football is built on a mistaken idea that they are out of pocket running football clubs. Even if this were true, so what? They put their money into clubs. *We* put our money into clubs. Nobody calls us saviours for our trouble, and if we decided that we'd had enough, we couldn't take our money with us if we walked away. Why all the fuss? When we were young, we were taught not to draw attention to our generosity, that virtue was its own reward. If we put money in a charity box we get a sticker for our trouble, and not the adulation of the public. For football chairmen that private satisfaction is not enough.

But any gratitude is more than most of them deserve. The owners and directors would like us to appreciate the contribution that they make by giving up their time to help the football club. They like to feel that they put money into football. But it is striking how often the flow of money goes the other way. It's not hard for directors to make money out of football. You do not have to be the chief executive of an élite club with all their commercial income. There are many ways of making money out of football. All sorts of clubs offer all sorts of means of making it worth while to become a director of a football club.

You can directly pay yourself a salary. You can employ yourself in your professional capacity. You can use the club to purchase goods and services from yourself. You can loan your club money at interest. You can fatten up the club by spending on fixed assets rather than players, so that the club, worth less on the pitch, is worth more when you resell it. (This was the policy which caused Norwich fans to have Robert Chase hounded out of Carrow Road.) You can flog off the ground for redevelopment. And most remunerative of all, you can float the club on the stock exchange, and see your holding in the club expand in value like a mushroom cloud. The money is there waiting to be made.

Before commercialisation, football clubs were run, day-to-day, by the club secretary, whose duties entailed paying invoices, rearranging postponed matches and writing to the county FA. All that has changed. Even smaller clubs seem to need chief executives, drawing good salaries regardless of the fortunes of their clubs. David Kohler has run Luton Town during one of the most disastrous decades of its history, but he continues in an agreeably salaried post. There are many better off than he. In August 1995, the magazine *Labour Research* listed six directors who were paid more than £100,000 a year. Two were at Chelsea, Ken

Bates and Colin Hutchinson, while the best paid of all, Bill Fotherby at Leeds, enjoyed a salary of almost a quarter of a million pounds a year.

Nice work if you can get it. If you can't, many other options are open to you. Clubs can have building work done by firms whose directors happen to be directors of the club. Swindon Town had a chairman who owned a business selling sports goods. The club shop sold his equipment. When Oxford were sold in 1992 the new board consisted of a group of lawyers. The club, mired in legal difficulties after Maxwell's death, needed legal representation and, of all the lawyers in the land, they felt that they themselves were the best people for the job. Southampton directors also selected themselves when choosing firms to carry out work for their club. They made, between them, a hundred and sixty thousand pounds in four years in recognition of their legal services, accounting services and building work. Not a fantastic sum, but nevertheless, an indication of the possibilities available.

It's easy for directors to take advantage of their position to advance their outside interests. There is nothing illegal about this, but it only heightens the impression of supporters that some directors feel the club is there to serve their interests rather than the other way round.

Loans are another source of easy profit. Bill Archer, at Brighton, made three hundred thousand pounds a year in interest out of a club which was, at that time, being relegated to the Third Division. David Evans 'put' money into Luton Town which helped them win the League Cup, raised his profile enough to help him into Parliament, and then resigned, taking back all his loans and all the interest on the top. Suddenly broke, Luton Town subsequently plummeted down the League. These are not atypical examples. It is not illegal to lend money to your football club and profit from the interest, but it cannot be squared with the image of the director as philanthropist.

There is money to be made out of football clubs, and there is money to be made from closing them, or moving them, or merging them. But if you really want to make an instant fortune out of football, there is no alternative to the stock market flotation. You only need to be a significant shareholder in a club at the moment that it's floated. One moment you've got nothing, and the next, you've made your fortune. When Southampton were the subject of a reverse takeover, the directors were awarded more shares for nothing, which, on flotation, caused the chairman's stake to rise in value from less than four thousand pounds to a million and a half. The other directors also made paper profits which amounted to more than a million apiece. Overnight they made a paper profit of forty five thousand per cent. When Leeds were taken over by the Caspian Group, the club's financial structure was similarly altered to benefit the directors on flotation. (On a different level, the takeover of Nottingham Forest, a restructuring rather than a flotation, allowed shareholders, whose shares were previously worth nothing, to sell those shares for five-figure sums.)

If these bonanzas are to have any merit, it will be if they persuade supporters that the goal of directors is not to help them out but to help themselves. Their main aim is to take more out than they put back in. There have been some spectacular successes. The £425,000 stake which Doug Ellis bought in Aston Villa, increased, on flotation, to £70 million. At Birmingham City David Sullivan made a paper profit of £4 million by spring of 1997. John Hall has bought Newcastle success, but he has bought himself a little bit as well, holding as he does an eighty per cent stake in a £200 million business. Ken Bates invested one whole pound in Chelsea. By February 1997 his stake was worth well over £50 million. If these people want to tell us that they're businessmen, and that their aim is just to make a profit, then let them stop posing as saviours and make it clear why they are in the game of football. Alan Sugar may not be a good thing for football, but he has one virtue, that he never claimed any motive for taking over Tottenham other than a desire to make some money out of them.

Do these people really deserve the fortunes that they've made out of the game? Have their clubs prospered so much that they are entitled to such generous rewards? Relative to their traditions, their potential and their expectations, have Birmingham prospered? Or Southampton? Or Forest, or Leeds? This may change, as clubs, like shares, can go up as well as down. But the contribution that their boards have made to any of these clubs is nothing compared to the contribution that they have made to themselves. Nor were directors responsible for the decline in hooliganism, or the invention of satellite television. Those factors, not the foresight of directors, are what made football, and football clubs, increase in financial value.

The enriching of directors is having its effect. At the same time as the mania for saviours has been growing, so has a mood of cynicism among many supporters about the motives of the boardroom. We are becoming interested not just in the club's performance but in the attitudes and interests of directors, and even success no longer necessarily buys them our respect. The contrast between those motives and those of the supporters, the difference between the treatment and the rewards of those in the stands and those in the directors' box, is making more supporters withhold their gratitude from those who don't deserve it.

Ken Bates is hardly universally admired at Stamford Bridge and nor is David Dein at Highbury. Even in Newcastle voices have been raised against John Hall, for bullying the local council into letting him put his new stadium where he wants it, rather than where it ought to be, regardless of the destruction of parkland and allotments that his plan entails.

Many supporters have had enough of this parade of greed and arrogance which passes for stewardship of our clubs. They question the loyalty of the people who run them. Many fans, when they think of their club, mentally separate that club from those who are in charge of it. When they think of what *they* mean by the club, they think of the fans, not the directors. They know that fans are permanent but directors are temporary. While the loyalty of fans remains as strong as ever, if loyalty is what motivates directors, it is remarkable how many of them are able to do what fans cannot, and transfer their loyalties from club to club.

Ken Bates started at Oldham long before he moved to Chelsea. Michael Knighton tried to take over Manchester United before settling for Carlisle. Victor Green left Hendon to move to Stevenage. Geoffrey Richmond cut his teeth at Scarborough before he moved on to greater things at Bradford City. Richard Thompson ran out of players to sell at QPR and went to Leeds instead. Peter Johnson did well at Tranmere but did even better for himself at Everton. Forest fans hope for better things from Irving Scholar than Tottenham fans were used to.

There are dozens of similar examples. We can either conclude that directors are like the Lone Ranger, roving the country looking for helpless football clubs to protect, or that being a club director, or a chairman, is a more desirable and more lucrative position than directors would have the fans imagine. There may be chairmen in the world who lose money. There may be directors who work desperately hard, with no more incentive than the desire to look after their football clubs. But compared to those who make a lot of money, to those who enjoy a lot of privileges, to those who hold their positions just because they have a mate upon the board, these selfless, hard-working directors seem to be thin upon the ground.

We cannot trust these people. There is too great a gulf between what we want from them and what they do, between the claims they make and the results that they achieve. But there is no replacing them with anybody better. The more football becomes a festival of greed, the less likely it is that clubs will be rescued by saints and philanthropists. We would be better off without the lot of them.

Even the white knights that so many hope for are not, in the final analysis, a good thing for the game. The sole accomplishment of high-spending chairmen has been to vastly increase the level of inflation in the game, to re-ignite the transfer market, to push up Premiership salaries even further, to increase the costs of football which are then inevitably paid for by the fans. If you are looking for Jack Walker's real legacy to football, you'll find it, not in the championship side of 1995, nor even in the rebuilt Ewood Park, but in ever more expensive ticket prices.

What Walker and his imitators bought, the fans have had to pay for. The best thing that could happen to the game would not be more Jack Walkers, but rather fewer. No more big spenders to push up the prices for us. No more philanthropists. And no more saviours. Football cannot afford them. It cannot handle many more saviours. It has been saved so often, by so many, that it may be almost past saving altogether.

5. THE MARKET PRICE

If anything is worse than having football treated as a rich man's plaything, it is the listing on the stock market which tends to follow. The last shreds of individual character in football, of football clubs as something particular and different, are being torn away. Football clubs are no longer measured in terms of goals and points and prizes. They are reduced to figures listed on the financial pages, and as their worth is measured by their ability to sell themselves to the City, they move even further away from the interests of their supporters.

In the short term, flotation on the stock market is a source of easy money, and therefore, like all such get-rich-quick schemes, it is likely to result in several instant fortunes for a few, and decades of regret for everybody else. Football is putting its entire future at the disposal of the stock market, and committing itself to play according to the rules of the casino. The values of the game are of no consequence. The values of the stock market count for everything. That market values nothing, save a short-term profit or a cast-iron certainty. If it takes a risk on you, it will do its best to make *you* pay for it. It brings about, and it encourages, gigantic differentials between rich and poor. It exerts its ruthless power to get exactly what it wants. For football, with its flimsy structure and its fragile finances, to place its destiny in the guardianship of the City of London is, in the long term, monumental foolishness.

But what is foolish for the many, may be wisdom for the few, and what is unwise in the long term, may be profitable in the short. In the first few years since football clubs resorted to the City, quick profits were, almost without exception, the result. The biggest beneficiaries may have been the lucky people in the boardroom, but almost everyone who bought shares in a football club, until the start of 1997, will have seen the value of their shares go up. Anybody who bought Manchester United shares in 1991 would have achieved a tenfold increase in their value in six years. Chelsea trebled in value in their first year on the market.

This success has not been limited to the élite clubs who have been successful on the pitch. Celtic won nothing in two seasons and still increased their value, over that time, by over 500 per cent. Leeds had to sack their manager, got nowhere near a qualifying place for Europe, and played the least attractive football in the country, and yet their shares did even better than did Chelsea's.

Some of these shares may have been undervalued at flotation, and the rises in the share values took place during a period when the stock market has generally boomed. But football's performance on the market has been out of all proportion. In four years, the FTSE-100 increased by 67 per cent, while the value of the quoted clubs increased by 700 per cent.

There were, of course, inflated expectations due to the market overestimating the potential of pay-per-view television, or because football shares, like football generally, were fashionable among yuppies who knew little about it and understood less. The market fell in early 1997, after Coopers and Lybrand issued a report suggesting that the sector, overall, was overvalued by a billion pounds. Shares fell in all listed clubs, which typically lost, between February and June 1997, around one third of theit market value. Yet although the value of some clubs, particularly Southampton, Sheffield United and QPR, fell in value by almost half, this didn't stop further flotations taking place.

Over the 1996-97 season clubs were coming to the market at the rate of almost one a month. By the end of that season 17 had listings either on the full stock exchange or on the Alternative Investment Market. Three clubs' shares were available on the Ofex market (Off the Exchange, meaning that neither financial information nor the shares themselves are as widely available as they would be with a stock market listing). The fashion appeared to have reached as far as Italy, as Milan and Juventus were reported to be considering flotations on the London stock market.

Advertisements appeared for something called The Football Fund, created by Singer and Friedlander, the investment bank. They were accompanied by Alan Hansen's photograph, and they invited us to hand over a thousand pounds, or 50 quid a month if we preferred, so that they could invest it in the game we love. Or so that we could make a bit of money out of it whether we love the game or not. This development was widely, and correctly, diagnosed as further evidence of the passing of the game into the hands of yuppies. We were accustomed to having football used as the vehicle for somebody else to make themselves some money, but never before had we been so enthusiastically encouraged to join in. It had never occurred to us before that the purpose of being a supporter was to make money from the game.

Share ownership in football clubs is nothing new. Most of us will know supporters who have owned football shares for many years, and few have done so with the intention, or the hope, of making money out of them. Supporters do not sell their shares. They buy them mainly to acquire a little piece of the club they love. Shares like that are a keepsake, not a trading card. During flotations, some of the people who buy shares are certainly supporters who are going to take exactly the same view, fans who would rather see their investment wearing a club shirt than coming back to them in dividends. That is the viewpoint of supporters who are shareholders. But it is not the viewpoint of major investors in football clubs.

For shareholders, the benefits of the boom are obvious. For supporters, they are not. It may appear that the millions of pounds added to the value of a club must mean money becomes available for new players, or for improvements to the ground. (Both Southampton and Newcastle floated their shares with their proposed new stadiums in mind.) Yet neither of these benefits are as straightforward as they might appear.

The brute fact is that most of the quoted clubs, those in the middle of the Premiership and those below, although they have increased their capitalisation by flotation, have fallen so far behind the élite clubs that even spending millions cannot begin to bridge the gap. And as other clubs join them on the market, their temporary advantage over more immediate rivals disappears. The potential for ground improvements is also an illusion. Investors don't buy into football clubs in order to make life more comfortable for supporters. They want to get their money back, which means those brand new seats will be a damn sight more expensive than the old ones, and that, ultimately, the supporters, not the investors, will have to pay for them. Supporters do not benefit from the influx of City cash. When Aston Villa came to market, Doug Ellis, expecting to raise £15 million immediately, promised the money would be spent on new players and ground improvements. But he also announced an increase in season ticket prices of 14 per cent.

That is what football on the stock market is all about. It only serves to make football more expensive. Investors expect a company to get the best price for its products that the market will bear. Football clubs are expected to charge supporters the highest price they can.

There is little that we can do to influence their decision. Certainly, buying shares gives us not one iota of control over our clubs, assuming we can actually afford to buy them. Aston Villa supporters had to find over £400 to make the smallest possible investment at flotation. Newcastle's sale was restricted solely to City investors and its season ticket holders. Supporters who were already priced out of the club now found they couldn't even buy themselves some shares in it. Once shares became freely available, of course, that situation changed – but by then the price had gone up. Effectively, the less you had to spend, the more you had to pay to buy yourself some shares.

After Margaret Thatcher promised to create a shareholders' democracy, share ownership actually became more unequal than it ever was before. The consequences in football are the same. Most football clubs had shareholders long before the stock market had anything to do with it, and shareholders had the right to attend the Annual General Meeting and put some faces to the names appearing on the masthead in the programme. The small shareholders usually constituted a minority shareholding and therefore their opinions, and votes, could safely be ignored. The situation now, if anything, is rather worse.

We still get a copy of the Annual Report, and the right to show up at the AGM, but now we are outnumbered far worse than before. The biggest shareholdings dwarf our puny votes. And they are more anonymous than they were before. These votes are cast by proxy, giving us no real idea who actually pulls the boardroom strings. We may know the names of the institutions, and even, if we are lucky, the names of the people running them. But we will not always know *who* they are, or what they want. Nor can we put the same pressure on them as we can an owner-chairman. You can organise meetings, and join in chants of 'Sack the Board'. But how can you shout Somebody Out when you don't know who that Somebody is, and when they are not at the game to feel the strength of the supporters' discontent?

There have been many absentee owners in football before. Bill Archer, at Brighton, and Robert Maxwell, at Derby, are two of the better-known examples. Oxford were owned for three years by a tax exile in Jersey who never attended any games, and whose name most supporters never knew. These were intolerable situations. Yet they promise in the future to be the rule rather than the exception, as ownership of football more and more resides within the Square Mile of the City. Football is already faceless enough without this further lurch into anonymity.

It all means that the balance between owners and supporters has shifted decisively towards the former. They are more powerful, more distant. Even the restrictions on dual ownership of clubs are now redundant, as investors spread their investments over a number of clubs. It is easy to see how someone with enough financial backing could manipulate the shares of more than one club so as to engineer whatever merger, or asset-stripping operation, they think they can get away with.

Football is at the mercy of these people. Kevin Keegan was forced out of Newcastle, not because of his failings as a manager, but because the club was ready for flotation. He was unsure if he wanted to stay at the club beyond the summer, and the City would not accept that uncertainty. Extraordinarily, the managership of a club was decided not by the preferences of the board (who wanted Keegan to stay) or even by the pressure of the fans, but by the City's silent pulling of invisible strings.

Apologists for the City argue that the better a football club performs on the pitch, the more it will attract City investors, thereby producing more success and further investment in a 'virtuous circle'. The argument is true in so far as lower division clubs do not attract investors and that clubs at risk of relegation usually see a wobble in their share price. In fact, even a single bad result can have a serious effect on a club's market value. When Wimbledon put Manchester United out of the 1997 FA Cup, £10 million came off their shares. The market performance of football clubs *reflects* their footballing performance. But it is an extremely distorted reflection. When share prices go up regardless of the fact that clubs are, by their standards, failing, the correlation, self-evidently, is extremely inexact.

The City has its own agenda. Investors are not looking for the same things as we are. Ticket prices are not the only obvious area of disagreement. The benefits of pay-per-view television are another. Exciting for the City, a real threat for supporters. Alan Sugar's stewardship of Tottenham demonstrates the difference in priorities between supporters and shareholders. In financial columns he is much praised. The club reports large and consistent profits. Their dividends are generous. In the stands, where fans pay just about the highest prices in the country, opinions are not so approving. By the end of 1996-97 it was six years since Tottenham had won a trophy. It was, indeed, several years since they even threatened to win one. Sugar was extremely frugal with his money. Where other clubs have spent, Sugar preferred to save. In 1996-97 there was no serious challenge even for a European place.

There are many clubs who do not expect to compete for top honours, and there have always been prominent clubs whose failures of management and internal disputes have prevented them from doing so. There have been boards at leading clubs whose sheer complacency has kept their clubs in relative mediocrity (the McKeag era at Newcastle, and the end of the McGinn dynasty at Celtic, fit this mould). But for a rich club to refuse to compete, *and then be praised for that approach,* is something new in football. Whatever strategy Tottenham opt for in the future, their mid-Nineties strategy consisted of little more than charging fans top whack in order to produce top dividends for rich shareholders.

'Investors don't really care what business they are in so long as the shares go up and the dividends come in.' So says Alan Sugar. The investors do not care about the game, and still less are they interested in style or pleasure in the game. All they want is a club whose fans will keep on pumping money into the club, and therefore into dividends, even if it loses. They want a sure thing, not a punt. In fact their views are often opposite to ours. On romantic principle, football fans usually support the small club against the big one. The City has neither principle nor romance. They back the powerful against the weak. There is nothing that we like to see more than a big club being knocked out of the Cup or relegated from the Premiership. There is nothing that the City enjoys less.

After the market wobbled following the Coopers and Lybrand report, the sector was reconstructed to the advantage of the biggest clubs. Not all clubs fell, like Southampton, by up to half their value. Manchester United lost only 11 per cent, and Sunderland a similar amount. Presumably the support of clubs like these was considered more rock-solid than that of QPR or Sheffield United. Patrick Haverson, in the *Financial Times,* described this as 'a flight to quality'. One might better describe it as a preference for certainty. Haverson continued, 'football on the stock market may just be coming of age'. That is one way to talk about it. Another is to wonder how on earth highly paid City analysts, paid to know more than us about the world we live in, could *ever* have put their money into any other than the biggest and most profitable clubs. Another is to wonder whether this trend to back only the larger clubs is really likely to be a good thing for football.

The City's contribution to the game is to make it less diverse, less interesting. Rather than making success possible, they make it harder, offering their money to the clubs who possess it already, depriving those who need it. The differentials between rich and small clubs, large enough already, are expanded to unbelievable proportions by the intervention of the stock market. Manchester United's value is twice that of Newcastle, maybe 20 times that of Southampton. It is an impossible situation. Clubs playing in the same division are operating with the sort of differences in their spending power which might have been the case 15 or 20 years ago between clubs playing their football three divisions apart.

What is the nightmare of supporters? It is football reduced to no more than a superleague, a handful of clubs, the same teams every year monopolising everything, able to charge fans impossible prices. That nightmare is the City's dream. Their influence in football can only be malign.

That influence is something we should fear. We ought to fear the impact on the game of the behaviour of the market. Entry to the stock market is supposed to force clubs to adopt a level of financial discipline which has been previously lacking in the boardroom. That may very well, as at Tottenham, be the case. But it is a straitjacket which the City itself is not prepared to wear.

While it insists, from others, on level-headed management and absolute consistency, it is the least level-headed, least consistent institution that you can imagine. It changes its mind half-a-dozen times a month. In one week in 1987 it wiped half the value off its shares, solely because it distrusted previous judgements it had made and chose to over-compensate by panicking. Its change of mind on football, in early 1997, may be just a foretaste. It can cut clubs down if it thinks it has paid out money it may not get back. The more competitive that football gets financially, the more that clubs will become overstretched. At that point, sooner or later, the City will panic, wipe millions off their value overnight and send them toppling over the edge. In the City there is no sense of shame, no sense of responsibility. There is only a determination to make others pay for the City's own mistakes.

In 1966 the City destroyed the economic policy of Harold Wilson. In 1992 it did the same to Norman Lamont and John Major. If it is prepared to bring down the policies of elected governments, is it likely to spare a thought before destroying football clubs? Football clubs are only of interest to the City as long as they produce consistent profits. Once they falter, it is easy to see how the City will demand multiple player sales, and much more, even up to the point of closing down a club. They like to hound Chancellors and finance ministers into doing their will. Football chairmen and managers will be easy meat.

What could we do about it? Very little. Football supporters are accustomed to a sense of helplessness. Putting control in the hands of the City only emphasises our lack of influence over the game we pay for. We are the servants, they the masters. Except that usually it is the master who pays the servant. In this case the financial relationship is the reverse. Essentially, we are paying the City for the right to have them frustrate our desires – and remake both clubs, and game, exactly in the image that they want them.

I do not think that this is what we want. I do not think that this is what is in the best interests of the game. But you cannot expect the City to be anything other than what it is. It is uncontrollable, manic, ruthless. When, in the future, it damages both our football clubs and football as a whole, there will be little mileage in complaining. We always knew what they were like. The only question will be why on earth our game was ever left in the care of people with the moral values of a shark.

6. ALL THAT IS HOLY IS PROFANED

The more football is sold, the less it is worth. Once football spreads itself too thinly, it becomes just another item of merchandise, flogged over and again for every last penny. In time it comes to mean a whole lot less. You cannot cover something in advertisements, and smother it with sponsors, and then assert that nothing's changed except the figure on the bottom line.

Not everything is measurable in money. If we were to measure football in that way, its wealth would be inversely proportional to its worth. But football, if it ever understood it, has forgotten that. Every new scheme to bring more money into the game, every additional encroachment of commercialisation, is taken without question to be beneficial. Each new sponsorship deal is hailed with press releases, promoted with photographs of handshakes. Figures are recited. Generosity is praised. Approving commentary is made. Prospects for the future are declared to be promising.

It is forgivable enough. A game accustomed to a hand-to-mouth existence is bound to revel in each new acknowledgement of its increased financial worth. Clubs who wage a permanent struggle against unequal odds are going to be relieved to find a sponsor prepared to offer a few quid for some tickets and some advertising. But that is nothing for supporters to rejoice in. Far from securing the future, commercial deals threaten it. Each one is another step along the road to perdition. Each new addition to the pile of money brings it closer to the moment when it topples over and crushes football underneath it.

It seems perverse to suggest that football should refuse money when it is offered. But the reasons to be sceptical become apparent when we ask exactly what that money does for us. What has all this commercial interest actually achieved? We should ask ourselves three questions. As a result of all the new money in football: is football cheaper for supporters? Is there any more of it? And has that money brought us better football? It is too easy, and too lazy, to assume that commercialisation is a good thing for the game. Ask it to justify itself, and it may turn out that rather than being beneficial, it is one of the major agents of the game's misfortunes.

Is football cheaper for supporters? Obviously it is not. The very time when commercial interests have become most involved in football has been the same time that football has become ruinously expensive. Indeed, the more successfully a football club markets itself, the higher the ticket prices it charges. Whatever happens to the money that comes into football, clearly none of it goes on cutting down the cost of football to supporters. It certainly cuts the cost of football for the sponsors, and the sponsors' friends and customers, since any sponsorship deal involves handing out a serious quantity of free tickets. But it achieves nothing for the supporters. No commercial deal ever took a penny off ticket prices.

Is there any more football than there used to be? There is not. There are the same number of professional clubs, in England and Wales, as there were before league sponsorship, before shirt sponsorship, before executive boxes and before they even allowed advertising hoardings round the pitch. Because commercialisation exacerbates the divisions between the rich clubs and the smaller clubs, the only contribution it has made is to help make it likely that the number of clubs will shrivel.

Nor are there any more competitions than there were before the age of sponsorship. They may create an unwanted and unnecessary European League within the next few years, but only at the cost of closing down the League Cup. The League, the FA Cup and the World Cup all survived and prospered for many decades without the help of sponsorship. In contrast to their longevity, whenever sponsors invent their own competitions, like the Texaco and Watney Cups of the Seventies, or the Makita International, nobody believes they matter, and nothing is more certain than the fact of their impermanence.

There is no more football than there used to be, because there is no genuine demand for it. If there was, it would have come to pass long ago, without the dubious aid of sponsorship to grease the wheels. And if football is any better for all the money that it's making, the evidence escapes me. It is no better as a game. Football is no more exciting because it's played in front of advertising hoardings. It is made no more thrilling by the adverts in the programme. The fans are no more passionate than they were, the crowd no more involved, the melodrama no more rousing. The fans do not yearn more to win a Cup because its title is extended to make room for the sponsors' name. If anything, the opposite is true.

Nor is the quality of football, for most of us, any better for all the commercial income in the game. The players we watch are much the same as they ever were. Conceivably, at the highest level, it might be claimed that Sharp helped bring Peter Schmeichel to Manchester United, that Carlsberg help keep Robbie Fowler at Anfield. But if it's the sponsors who are paying for the superstars, supporters might wonder what *their* money's paying for. Why the enormous ticket price if the sponsors are picking up the tab? They should not be fooled. They have very little for which they should be grateful to the sponsors.

Commercialisation does nothing for supporters. Its only contribution to our costs is to increase them. And it ensures that football is unable to stand on its own two feet, makes it dependent on funding from outside. It therefore forces football to become the property of someone else. Football dances to someone else's tune. That is the nature of commercial sport. The purpose of the spectacle is not the spectacle itself but the advertising opportunities that it provides. Its major preoccupation becomes the sale of itself.

Commercialisation takes on a life of its own. More and more of a club's time becomes devoted to the provision of commercial opportunities, to corporate hospitality and a hundred different forms of advertising. If these are sufficiently successful, *they* become the purpose of the club. The fact that it is a *football* club becomes merely a backdrop to the wining-and-dining circuit which moves on in the summer to Wimbledon and the Tests.

Sometimes football shows signs of shame at selling itself so eagerly. But it goes ahead and does it all the same. When the Football Association, knowing they should not be doing it, sold off the FA Cup to Littlewoods, they didn't even have the guts to do it properly. The Cup sort of retained its name, sort of rejected a change of title, and became 'the FA Cup, sponsored by Littlewoods'. If the name was going to be inviolate, then why was the competition not? If the FA were proud to sell the Cup to Littlewoods, why be so apologetic? There was no reason why the FA Cup needed to be sold to anyone, for any price. And it is hard to tell which is preferable, the shamelessness of Old Trafford, where everything is for sale and none of it is cheap, or the hypocrisy of Lancaster Gate, which sells its most prized possession without needing to and then can't make up its mind whether it should have sold it. One side understands only that football is for sale. The other secretly knows it shouldn't be, but goes ahead and sells it anyway.

Everything is for sale. The insistence on selling everything available spoils everything. It has made a billboard of the football shirt. The most cherished symbol in the game, the object of much pride to supporters, the shirt's integrity was doomed once marketing departments realised how sellable it was. It has suffered enough from being redesigned and revamped by people who didn't understand that the whole point of club colours was that they needed to be strong and to be traditional. All sorts of designer detritus has been added to it. They have discovered how to relaunch and relaunch it in order to bully parents into buying it again and again.

But once they grasped the fact that the shirt represented a million walking billboards, and that it offered a 90-minute advert to the television audience, the shirt was destined for permanent humiliation. The colours, and the badge, are dominated by the sponsors' names, as if Tottenham *were* Hewlett Packard, or Arsenal JVC.

Once we identified a football team by the recognition of its colours. Now we recognise the sponsor's name and thereby recognise the football team. We wouldn't pay to advertise these companies, but we have no option if we wish to wear a football shirt. That is the nature of the relationship between football and commerce. Commerce forces itself on football, unasked and unrequired, and subordinates the game to its own requirements.

Football used to reject the advances of commercial interests precisely because it feared the consequences of allowing them to dictate to football and because it considered there was substance and importance to its traditions and integrity. You do not have to go back very far to find photographs of players wearing shirts that carry no more extraneous matter than a number and a badge, photographs of football grounds in which the football pitch and stands are not separated by rows of advertising boards. Even into the Seventies, the directors of Tottenham refused to allow advertising boards into the ground. Now, of course, White Hart Lane is a shrine to the commercialisation of football.

Other grounds are catching up. At least Tottenham's ground still has the dignity of keeping its own name. Scarborough play at the McCain Stadium, Huddersfield at the Alfred McAlpine Stadium, Bolton at the Reebok Stadium. Valley Parade has disappeared. The Pulse Stadium has taken its place. The Shrivenham Road becomes the Intel Stand. We are not even allowed to keep our names any more. Commercialisation has taken away our identity.

You cannot sell everything you have and then claim that at least you have your pride. Not when your pride is among the things that you have sold. It makes a difference. Pride is important, irreplaceable, in football. There are many reasons why this is true. Many supporters look to football for a sliver of pride to set against the regular humiliations they suffer in their lives. It makes it all the more important to hang on to the small symbols of pride we have, from the colours of the shirt to the identities of name.

It is a very slippery slope that we are on. Rugby League has got in the habit of giving its clubs inappropriate titles – the Rhinos, the Vikings, the Bulls – in the style of American Football teams. No doubt this indignity, too, will be heaped on supporters before too long, and we shall have the pleasure of watching the Chelsea Chargers, or the Ipswich Hawks. Making me watch the Oxford Students would be more than I could bear. But if adopting stupid names might make it easier for clubs to sell themselves, then that is what they're going to do.

It is hard for football to retain its sense of pride. It becomes even harder because of all the bowing and scraping that it has to do to the sponsors. Club sponsors, match sponsors, matchball sponsors. All have to be thanked for their generosity, in the programme, and on the PA. Of course they are not doing it for nothing. Sponsors become sponsors out of commercial calculation, not from generosity or sentiment. They are paying for advertising, a higher profile and free tickets into the bargain. But we have to grovel to them like a bellboy accepting a tip.

Those are the ethics which prevail in football. The fans, who do not benefit from sponsorship, are expected to applaud the sponsors, who do. Sponsorship is institutionalised hypocrisy for clubs, supporters and for players. When players speak their minds they get in trouble for it. Robbie Fowler was fined for wearing a T-shirt supporting the sacked Liverpool dockers. Yet players are expected to implicitly endorse the sponsors – or even explicitly, by attending promotional functions and meeting the sponsors' guests after the game, whether they admire their companies or not. Approval that is not given freely is a lie. Sponsorship is a lie.

Yet that lie dominates the mind of football. It cannot wait to lie as often, as expensively, as possible. That is the way sport behaves nowadays, and football is no different to any other. To its supporters it is totally different. But in commercial eyes it is not. It is just part of the circuit. It is another advertising opportunity. It makes no difference to the advertisers whether that opportunity be found in football, or rugby, or something else entirely.

But I did not become a football fan because it was no different to anything else. The very idea was that football *was* different, was a world apart. Not to be different is to be disposable. To the advertiser placing their logo on a shirt, it makes no difference what sport the shirt derives from. The only difference is the price. Commercialisation is a process in which everything becomes the same, merely filling different places on a satellite television schedule. They merge into each other, resemble one another. And since their purpose is to provide an audience for the same advertisers, their purpose is the same.

Our pride, integrity and in several ways our identity is being eroded by commercialisation. It would have been better if it had never been allowed to intrude into football in the first place. It is too late to turn the clock back. Of course we need to stand up to its influence, to struggle against the indignities it heaps upon us, to resist its most insidious effects. But it is highly unlikely that we can do what would be actually desirable, which would be to extirpate it totally.

Yet it does not hurt to think about it. We take commercial interference for granted. There is much in football that we take for granted, and most of it is unnecessary. All we need, to watch our football, is a park, some players and a set of stands to watch them from. Everything else is extraneous. In principle sponsorship is totally unnecessary to football. We tolerate it. We should tolerate it less.

It makes a lot of money. But it does not make that money for us. That money is not used for our benefit. It does not benefit the game of football. What good is it to us? It is time football remembered what it is worth, what it is worth to us, what it is worth as football, and not what it is worth as a commercial opportunity to people who do not give a damn about the game.

7. THE VICIOUS SPIRAL

What matters to supporters is the football, not the money that it generates. Once that principle is laid aside, it is nearly impossible to get it back. Profit is not an easy bandwagon from which to descend. Yet the faster that bandwagon rolls, the more people are able to clamber aboard. The more people there are who draw their salaries from commercial activities, the more who draw their dividends from an increase in income, the more there are whose vested interest lies in football as a business rather than football as a game.

Yet if all the money in football never seems to make it any healthier, if it only serves to make its crisis worse, the main reason is not the growing layer of people who are taking out their slice and putting nothing in, but the normal economic circumstances of professional football. These circumstances ensure that no increase in its income, however great, serves to resolve its difficulties. Pouring more money into the game is like putting out a fire with paraffin. It cannot help. Demonstrably, it has not helped. And it can only make the problems worse that it was intended to solve.

Where does the money go? Some goes straight out of the game to directors and speculators. But most goes straight out of a club, to other clubs as transfer fees, to players as wages. The more that comes in, the quicker it goes out. What football makes, it spends. Not because the game is run by spendthrifts – most fans are generally inclined to think their board too parsimonious – but because the demands of professional football leave it with no choice. Football spends money because it must.

The cause of this compulsion is competition. Competition *within* competition. Within the outer framework of a free market economy, clubs compete with each other economically. This system would be designed to swiftly put most clubs out of existence were it not for the loyalty of supporters who, unlike investors, are prepared to back a loser rather than a winner. Football creates more losers than it does winners and it punishes those losers financially. Clubs that fail are made to know they've failed through reductions in their revenue. Football is a permanent, daily fight for income, a fight which is only won by making others lose.

Professional football reproduces all the features of a market economy in the most manic manner. What distinguishes it from most other areas of economic activity is that in this market most of the winners are those who sell their labour power, not the purchasers.

Of course, for most of those employed within the game this is a travesty of the truth. Football relies on cheap labour. It thrives on it. Most clubs rely on voluntary work and unpaid hours by fans and employees. Top Premiership clubs, with turnovers in the tens of millions, employ programme sellers and turnstile operators on money not much better than a child gets for a paper round. Clubs that can find millions to pay their leading players employ youth players on YTS schemes.

They get away with it because the Government allows them to. But they also get away with it because they play on the loyalty of supporters who, for the greater glory of their club, will work for nothing, and on the hopes of teenage players, each of whom will gamble their future, for no return, on the one chance in a hundred that they will make a fortune out of football.

It is a cruel, exploitative, a manic and a fickle system. Fans have a reputation for being fickle. But everybody in the game is fickle when rewards are great, but at the same time everybody's future can depend on a referee's decision, or a deflection, or a moment's lapse in concentration. There is an omnipresent fear of failure, and in that fear lies football's cruelty and its anger. It is extraordinary, when you think about it, that some of the most highly paid people in society, people who are gods on the pitch and aristocrats at home, are spoken to at work in a manner that convicted criminals would find intolerable coming from a prison officer. Millionaires are screamed at, sworn at and humiliated. Their working life is mostly one of arbitrary command and public criticism.

But, treated as slaves as they may be, the butt of everybody's anger, the best paid people in the game are the professional players and their managers. They are in a position to make football pay them what they want. The higher up the game you go, the more true this becomes. Clubs chase players rather than players hawking themselves round clubs. It is a permanent bidding war and no one can afford to let their rivals win.

Football clubs are in the same situation as factory owners who must invest in new machinery or give way to their competitors. Except that players are less reliable performers than machines. They also wear out more quickly, and unlike machines, they can move from one company to another of their own free will. Yet they are, essentially, the only factor in production. Everything depends on them and everything can go wrong so quickly. So while football is a labour-intensive industry, with all the inevitable desire of the directors to cut labour costs, it has, nevertheless, no real way to do so. Clubs want to cut costs, yet cutting costs instantly reduces their performance.

Therefore they are under a constant pressure to make changes and, rather than cut, they have to spend. Players are in the weakest position possible to demand a long-term contract, but in the strongest position possible to demand the highest wages that they can. Baulk at their requirements and some other club will offer them another five hundred pounds a week. These are skilled workers. They are not easily replaceable.

There is no real wage restraint in football. Bill Shankly and Matt Busby secretly agreed between them not to offer increased wages to players at either of their clubs. But that sort of agreement would be impossible now. Clubs only have the bluff, the threat, and the lie left in their armoury. Players can be browbeaten by bullies, or can be offered promises that clubs have no intention of fulfilling. But given proper representation, players are able to get most of what they want. Clubs are not in a position to say otherwise.

Clubs have to spend and spend as much as possible. If their performance improves because their spending works out well, then they move up to a higher level where they have to spend even more. If they refuse to spend more, then their players find a club that will, and leave. Youth policies do not solve the problem for long. You still have to pay the players a salary appropriate to their level. So clubs cannot stop spending. Every injection of new cash tends to be swallowed up by the market. New income cannot be set aside for long. If more money is made from television, or new sponsorship deals signed, or ticket prices increase even more, that money has to be spent. If more money comes into football, players can simply ask for more and get it. If one club doesn't spend its extra income, another club will, and they will get the players both clubs want.

The Premiership is making a lot of money, but it has to spend it. The *Investors Chronicle* estimates that over the first five years of its existence, Premiership wages went up by an average of 22 per cent a year. An average first-team player at an average Premiership club can expect to make £5,000 or so a week. That, in itself, is twice the wages top Arsenal players were paid for winning the Championship in 1989.

It is a carousel of ever-increasing speed. Money greases its wheels and the more money there is, the faster that it spins. Its effect is almost entirely inflationary. In industry, an increase in revenue may be re-invested to create new plant, and new production, to employ more people who receive and spend some of that money. In football, a rise in income is not productive in this way. It creates nothing new, brings about no increase in production. Some of the money might be spent on ground improvements, but clubs' performance on the field usually suffers if they spend money anywhere else. Even if it did not, the scope for diverting expenditure in that direction is obviously finite. New money stays in football, there is no more football created in consequence, and the outcome, therefore, is inflation.

Every increase in income translates itself into an increase in costs. Even if the Bosman judgement cuts down transfer fees, the ultimate result will be a proportionate increase in signing-on fees. The purchase of players from overseas may depress the market for a time, but if this proves to be an advantage then everyone will do the same, and over time overseas players' wages will rise to much the same level as domestic wages. In the long term there is no escape.

It will not do to blame the players. Like any other employees, they are simply asking for the highest proportion of their company's income that they can. If this was not perfectly understandable at the best of times, it certainly is when other people are treating football as a honeypot. The system, not the players, makes these problems impervious to increases in football's income. It is the uncontrollable market which gives football clubs no option but to chase each other at an ever faster pace down the blind alley of the transfer market.

Of course there is not a perfect and immediate correlation between increasing income and increasing costs. Any club can get ahead of the game for a while by buying the right players, employing the right manager and thereby bringing in more supporters.

But even if it gets over the hurdle of increased costs that comes in the wake of success, it also has to contend with having raised supporters' expectations. It has to repeat its success all over again. Sooner or later money must be spent, or interest, and therefore income, will slip.

Profitability can only be short term. Football is an economic system in which almost nobody can make a steady profit. All clubs make a profit at one time or another, but in the long term all have to compete by spending more than their income. Only the transfer system, in enabling them to recoup their losses, keeps most football clubs in business. Long-term profitability is a chimera, a dream to which all football clubs aspire but which almost none can attain.

There are a few exceptions to this rule. Some of the élite clubs may find themselves able to maintain consistent profits. Because nobody can outspend them, they do not have to exhaust their profits in the race to get ahead. Because their income dwarfs that made by other clubs, they have some breathing space. If your turnover is twice that of your rivals, you don't have to offer twice their wages to get the players you want. Half as much again may suffice, and still leave a big slice for the shareholders. Nor do these clubs suffer from the same problem of increasing costs by rising to a higher level. There is no higher level.

It is not quite as easy as that. Only one of these teams can win the Premiership each season. These clubs do compete with each other but that is rather easier than having to compete with 20 different clubs and then, if you succeed and get promoted, having to do it, at increased cost, all over again. This may change. The élite already compete with top European clubs for players. When a European League begins, that competition will be more serious. Top players will command salaries similar to US basketball players, while the *domestic* élite will no longer be able to guarantee success. Nor, therefore, could they guarantee the sort of income which enables them to pay their players top whack and still leave plenty over for the shareholders. They will try to avoid these problems. When the European League emerges, the Manchester Uniteds of the world want to keep playing in their domestic leagues as well. They want the riches on offer from European TV coverage without risking losing the cushion that they get from guaranteed success.

But those few clubs which are becoming safe from the clammy hand of debt are passing that same burden, severalfold, on to the rest of football. The fact that they are able to outspend the rest of football doesn't mean that rest of football is exempted from attempting to catch up. Other clubs have to go some of the way towards matching the salaries that the élite clubs can pay their squad players. Otherwise those players will remain squad players rather than coming to smaller clubs, even smaller clubs in the Premiership, as first team players.

The wages spiral continues apace and the effects are felt right the way down to the lowest levels of professional football. Like a train in which each carriage pulls the one behind, every level has to try and keep up with the one above it, dragged along by the engine of the economic success of the élite clubs.

The financial obligations of all football clubs are increasing and this is only paid for by increasing the financial obligations of supporters. So we go round and round, watching the same standard of football at ever-increasing cost to the people who pay to watch it.

The faster this inflationary spiral is made to work, the more it comes under intolerable strain. The benefits of the boom are mostly felt at the top, while the burdens it creates are largely felt by those who have not felt the benefits. The bulk of the money is pouring in at the top, yet the costs are increasing all along the line.

You would expect a league system, ranking clubs as if they were on a ladder, to pay its players in some similar fashion, each level paying a little higher than the one above. But the wages of average Premiership players can enormously exceed those paid to good players of almost equivalent ability in Division One. The League clubs do not have the television revenues that would enable them to match those salaries. The system is skewed out of all recognition. Clubs that want to keep their players have to pay them now in the hope of making up the deficit later. The risks increase, yet the rewards become ever less equally distributed, ever more unattainable for those who take the risks. We cannot go on like this indefinitely.

Even within Premiership clubs the potential for strain is obvious. Those average salaries pale in comparison to what the most sought-after players are receiving. Wage structures are coming under increasing pressure. We can easily imagine the internal ructions within teams whose players receive vastly unequal rewards for their efforts. Arsenal have been struggling for some years with this dilemma, opting out of the race for most top European players for fear of the impact on their wage structure, yet at the same time painfully aware that eventually their policy will cause them to fall behind. These ructions, these dilemmas, reflect the fissures that are opening up in football generally as we realise that all the boom has brought, for most, is inflation and insecurity. Any society that becomes increasingly unequal becomes dysfunctional, riven by discord, by anger, by feelings of injustice and ingratitude. Football, which has spent the last ten years seeking inequality and getting it, is starting to break down as a result.

We have to find a way to control the uncontrollable. The economics of football are designed to put clubs out of business. Only the loyalty of the fans prevents the game tearing itself to bits, and there is only just so much that we can do. Some way has to be found to stop football clubs spending what they choose regardless of the consequences, some way to stem the flow of money. Clubs cannot be forced, cannot be left, to carry on the struggle on their own. We need somebody to enforce the interests of the game over the interests of the individual club.

Football fans are not used to showing such perspective. Football encourages us to think about our club and not to think about the game in general. Divisions between us are basic to the game's existence. But it is now a time for vision and for foresight. The game is sinking, under its own economic rules, under the weight of its own income. Either we can sink or we can find a way to swim together. Otherwise we will have sold the present, only to find out that there may be no future at all.

8. MOVING THE GOALPOSTS

The Bosman judgement may be the straw that breaks the camel's back. At the very time that football clubs are forced to spend money as never before, the judgement, and the subsequent collapse of part of the transfer market, makes it far riskier for them to do so because it makes it harder, far harder, for them to get their money back. A vital prop of football's economic structure has been knocked away.

Football desperately needs to respond to the new situation. Yet anything it does is likely to be too little and too late, because, as the judgement further exaggerates the differentials between football clubs, it merely emphasises the divergence in their interests. The damage to the game could only be reduced by taking from those whose power has been much increased by the judgement, and who, therefore, will neither want nor need to help out the rest of football. The judgement may bring chaos but in a situation of chaos it is every man for himself. And every man for himself is a policy that suits the interests only of the biggest and most powerful.

The judgement will not destroy the transfer system altogether. But already, along with the ending of the restrictions on cross-border movements of professionals within the European Union, it has brought about the near-evaporation of the flow of transfer money from the Premiership to the League. One estimate suggests that since the rules were changed that flow has reduced to only ten per cent of what it was before. That is the outline of an imminent catastrophe.

Moreover, talking about Bosman, we may as well assume that the transfer system *is* about to cease to exist. Small football clubs are having to make that assumption, to anticipate no transfer income when planning their expenditure. In addition, the judgement *ethically* opposes the transfer of players for money on the basis of the free movement of labour, and therefore forces us to discuss whether the system actually should exist. Let start by assuming that the transfer system *is* basically finished. That way we can more clearly understand the risks that football clubs are being made to run, and we can discern, behind the real and justified fight for the rights of employees, another struggle to make sure that the dice are loaded even further in favour of the rich and powerful.

The transfer system rests on two relationships – the relationship between a football club and the players it employs, but also the relationship between two different football clubs. The second of these relationships makes the transfer system vital to the structure of the game, something which cannot be removed without the most profound and painful, and possibly fatal, changes to that economic edifice, because it is the only real mechanism for redistribution that the game possesses.

It is a practical question as well as an ethical one. We have already seen that football needs that redistributive mechanism by virtue of its basic economics. The issue is necessity, not husbandry. Football is a struggle between economic agents of vastly unequal size, in which most clubs are required by force of circumstance to spend beyond their means. That is why clubs are often referred to as selling clubs or buying clubs. Without the machinery of transfers, the selling clubs would gradually be destroyed. Without it they are, effectively, forbidden to compete. Without the lubrication that the existence of transfer fees provides, the economy of football will seize up.

You do not have to like the system, or its restriction on the rights of employees, to see why it is crucial to preserve the beneficial effects which it has on football. Nor do you have to disagree with the judgement to choke on some of the support which it attracted. No sooner was the judgement made than John Hall declared his undying support for the rights of professional players and his profound disagreement with the buying and selling of players. John Hall's public prominence is due to the purchase of many players for his football club. His wealth was not acquired without the use of low-paid and non-union labour, a process in which concern for the right of employees was not the obvious motive. His club, of course, might hope that the judgement will deliver, as free transfers, the sort of players for whom they had been paying millions.

Still, whatever questionable and self-seeking support it might have collected, considering only the relationship between a player and their club, the judgement was entirely right. It *is* intolerable that any individual, at the end of their contract, should be prevented by their employer from moving to whatever job they feel like.

It is common knowledge now that Jean-Marc Bosman was abominably treated by a football club that deprived him of his basic rights out of nothing more than spite. Perhaps the system in England and Wales would have protected him. But it is still unreasonable to expect players to put their futures in the hands of their employers. The level of protection that they have was achieved only relatively recently, when the retain-and-transfer system was abolished. That victory was only won in the teeth of opposition from the clubs. That has been true of every advance that players have been able to achieve. The abolition of the maximum wage was not all that very long ago.

Football clubs are not entitled to expect employees to settle for fewer rights than anyone else, nor ask them to be sacrificial victims in the cause. They do so too often already, making life difficult for players who take action in the courts when they suffer injuries that threaten their careers. It is up to football to decide how it should sensibly be run, not up to players to go without because it isn't.

From that perspective the transfer system seems to be unjust, however vital it may be to football. Yet when we look at it as a relationship between one club and another, removing it would be the greater injustice. Getting rid of the transfer system is a swindle in the making.

If rich clubs become able to sign players from other clubs for nothing, that is a scam. It is, quite simply, the exploitation of others' financial weakness in order to acquire assets for nothing. It is allowing one set of people to put in a lot of work, then another set to grab all the rewards. Football is a world of different exploitations, of players exploited by their clubs, of supporters exploited by their clubs. Taking away the transfer mechanism will only add another, clubs exploiting clubs, to that extensive list.

If constructive work is to be rewarded in society then football clubs are entitled to some return as well. They contribute to the economic value of their players. If a player leaves a club a better player than he joined, more sought after, more likely to enhance the prospects of a major club, his own hard work and application is not the only factor. Good coaches develop players. Good coaches make bad players into good ones. Brian Clough was a genius not because he won two European Cups but because some of the players with whom he did it shouldn't even have kept him in the First Division.

Dario Gradi has revitalised a football club by consciously producing players for the transfer market. Transfer fees are his, and the club's, reward. Over his time at Gresty Road, Crewe have produced no end of players for the ultimate benefit of larger clubs, of whom Rob Jones and David Platt are merely the most famous. At the same time, they are two promotions to the good. That is good football management. It should not be made impossible to repeat. At buying clubs, the transfer system may be a way out for a failing manager, able to buy a new player every time the previous buy turns out to be unwise. But at selling clubs, most clubs, transfer fees are recognition and reward for good planning and successful coaching.

These fees are not some racket, some way of protecting the inefficient from the consequences of their failures. Over the last ten years no top division club has had to sell as many players as have Wimbledon. Is that because they're inefficient? It would be fun to watch John Hall run a football club on Wimbledon's budget. It is, rather, a testament to their *efficiency*, to their ability, to the success of their managers in making internationals out of very ordinary players. Wimbledon have become a lot more popular in the last couple of years. As the élite clubs have become ever more bloated, their own status as a small fish among sharks has become more appreciated. But with no transfer market there could have been no Wimbledon. Without that market there could be no Crewe.

The Bosman judgement did recognise that clubs were owed some payback for their contribution to the development of players. It recommended some sort of compensation fee be paid to clubs whose players move to other clubs before the age of 24. It is not much of a bargain. It is hard to see what good that is to clubs whose players reach their middle twenties before their promise is revealed. Matt Elliott left Oxford for the Premiership at the age of 28. I saw Peter Shilton play a Cup-tie at the age of 47. Without the transfer market, he would not have commanded a transfer fee since Ted Heath was Prime Minister.

Shilton, who played in a World Cup semi-final at the age of 40, may be an exceptional example, but Elliott is not. Players do not cease to develop as professionals in their middle twenties. They do not cease to learn. Managers and coaches do not cease to teach them. There is no logical reason why the principle of compensation should be revoked at the age of 24. If it is due to clubs for their contribution to the development of players, why cut it off at 24? If it is not, why offer compensation in the first place?

It is stone cold certain that whatever compensation is on offer will never be enough to make up for the money smaller clubs will have lost in transfer income. It might even make the situation worse. It has, for instance, been proposed that clubs be compensated on a scale proportionate to the value they themselves place on a player. In other words, the more they paid a player, the more generous his contract, the greater the fee to which they would be entitled.

This is similar to how a transfer tribunal works now. But given that smaller clubs cannot afford anything like the wages that Premiership clubs can pay, the danger would be that smaller clubs would have to pay far more to buy a player from the Premiership than they would receive for the same player if they were selling him! Work it the other way round – have the buying club pay compensation proportionate to the wages they wish to pay – and that might be more to the point. But that, in its turn, would probably be unfair to the players.

Compensation will probably be risible and the situation will get worse as the richer clubs exert their power to secure their interests. This is illustrated by the decision to bring domestic transfers (in the Premiership, at least, with the League likely to follow shortly) into line with the Bosman judgement from the 1998–99 season. Out-of-contract players aged 24 and over will move without a transfer fee and without compensation. From which we can see two things – that smaller clubs will lose transfer income that they presently enjoy, and that we are moving away from real compensation, not towards it. Compensation will only be payable for players 23 and under, and we can bet that it will not make up for what clubs lose in transfer fees. And the longer we go before it is statutory, the worse the arrangement is likely to get. John Hall is certainly not going to start proposing that he pays compensation where currently he may have to pay nothing, whether that compensation be paid directly or via some sort of central fund. The more they find their position further strengthened by the Bosman judgement, the more the élite clubs are likely to take advantage of the fatalism that the judgement has had on smaller football clubs, to realise how incapable of acting in unison these clubs are and to resist anything that hints at taking money off them to help the clubs who need it.

After the judgement was made, there was some brief panic among the élite when they wondered if they might lose, for nothing, what had cost them millions to buy. But they have absolutely nothing to fear. If their top players can leave for nothing, other top players can join for nothing too. Not that they often have to sell for nothing. Few players leave top clubs on free transfers, except retiring players and players on the fringes of their squads. Most of their players are extremely sellable, give or take their wage demands. For these clubs, the fear of losing their expensive players only means that it would be wise to think about selling their players, all of whom are in demand, before their contracts actually expire. In an age where the best players expect to move from country to country as a matter of course, stopping at clubs for only two or three years at a time, that isn't going to make a lot of difference.

For all we know, the transfer system may *not* necessarily survive in any recognisable form. Paying money for human flesh may become socially unacceptable. Professional players may find themselves giving notice, just like other people do. But for the moment at least, some sort of transfer system will continue. Before a contract ends, a player will still not have the automatic right to move wherever he may please, and so a fee will continue to be payable when a move is arranged. The transfer market will remain an everyday part of football. If two different clubs are interested in a player who isn't out of contract, they will still have to offer transfer fees. If clubs offer their players longer contracts, or renew them earlier, the question of a free move need not often arise. Players, aware of the dangers of injury and of the fact that clubs will not usually wait for them, do not take the risk of turning down a contract extension just because another club *may* still want them in six months or a year. Generally, they will sign, and free agency will become more rare.

In principle this is a good idea. It protects the vulnerable employee who stands to lose his livelihood. But it will be the smaller clubs, who can least afford to offer these extensions, who will have to do so most often. Nor will the fees that they receive be nearly as high as they are today. The collapse in lower-division transfer income is the proof. The reasons are twofold. The first is that clubs will find themselves under more pressure to sell cheaply if they fear that players out of contract may otherwise leave for nothing. The other is that as Bosman worsens the financial position of the smaller clubs, their more vulnerable financial position will force them to settle for much less than they would have got before. The bank will not let these clubs hang on till they get the best price they can.

The main result of the Bosman judgement has been a redistribution of wealth and influence to the richest clubs and to the richest players. This is not the fault of Jean-Marc Bosman. It is the fault of football for allowing itself to splinter into rich and poor.

The Bosman judgement is not the sole reason for the splintering of football, but it is probably the most important. It takes away the most important means we had of alleviating all the other damage caused to football in the last few years. It is a sign of the state football has fallen into, that allowing its employees the same civilised rights as anybody else should be a major threat to its survival. Yet that blow for fairness and equality is likely to rebound to the advantage of inequality and unfairness.

It doesn't have to. Many fairer systems could be devised than either the one we have had or whatever is likely to replace it. But unless the game is forced to recognise its obligations, to come to some arrangement which genuinely protects the incomes of the smaller clubs, something more than a token compensation payment, then the judgement has set them on the road to bankruptcy, or insignificance, or both. We know that most of us want nothing of the sort to happen. But who will act to prevent the otherwise inexorable? Rich clubs will not. Smaller clubs cannot. The fans might, if we had some power. But as it is we have no option but to look on as football slowly disintegrates, victim perhaps of outside forces, but also victim, crucially, of its own wilful and doltish lack of vision.

9. BUY NOW, PAY LATER

Football is playing in the unspoken shadow of increasing debt. Debt stalks the lower divisions, just as it has always done, but worse than before. At the same time, its shadow is beginning to fall on clubs much higher up the league than those who are its usual victims. Football is storing itself up a problem with which, sooner or later, it is going to have a painful reckoning.

In the middle of an economic boom in football, clubs in the Premiership might appear to have the opposite problem: how to spend their money, rather than where to find it. Indeed, as these clubs continue to enjoy some of the benefits of the boom, they may think themselves safe, in the future, from the problems with which they struggled in the past. Yet cracks are showing in the façade of optimism. Manifestations of growing pessimism are beginning to emerge.

One is the Premiership requesting to reduce the number of relegation places to two. Another is the wobble in the stock market. A third is the failure of some clubs, even after their flotation on the stock market, to be prepared to spend much of their increased capital. Both Sunderland's relegation in 1997, and Graeme Souness' resignation, in which he criticised Southampton's spending policy, seem to point to an increased nervousness in some Premiership boardrooms. Some clubs who expected to do well out of the Premiership are becoming nervous of its consequences and are hoping to avoid the ever-present obligation to spend. Of course, any individual club may change direction, swap a policy of caution for a policy of risk. But it seems clear that even top division clubs do not feel the same confidence in the future as they did in the initial euphoria, at the beginning of the Premiership.

Nobody really knows how football stands financially. Inflation of both prices and wages has become so rife, the financial whirligig so fast, that all published figures are out of date before we see them. Nor are those figures intrinsically reliable. Year-on-year figures for profit and loss do not tell supporters very much. A paper profit often means only that a club has had a year of enforced player sales, probably preceded by a year of heavy losses, and likely followed by the same, as the effect of selling players proves to be a decline in both playing and financial performance. Even the bottom line, the club's balance of assets set against its debts, is not a perfect guide to the club's status. Flotation can make it swing dramatically one way and collapse on the stock market can make it swing dramatically the other.

Moreover, clubs' financial crises are rarely public knowledge until those clubs are almost on the brink. They come to our attention overnight, when creditors are already moving winding-up petitions, administrators already being called upon to determine whether a club can be saved. Financial crisis always appears intermittently and therefore always appears to be a consequence of the particular mistakes and policies of any one particular club. Yet we can detect a deeper pattern, a pattern suggesting a general and growing problem in the game.

One sign of a mounting problem in the background is that the debts which clubs reveal during crises are higher than they ever were before. The two major crises of 1996-97 involved Bournemouth and Millwall. In the same week in January, Millwall called in administrators, Bournemouth the receivers, and the latter, fighting off a number of winding-up petitions, came extremely close to closure. They owed, in total, close to five million pounds, which for a team playing in Division Two, and turning over in turnstile income about a million pounds a season, is an astronomical figure.

Yet Millwall's debts, inflated by the building of a new stadium, some unwise business deals and an attempt to reach the Premiership which backfired, were over twice the figure Bournemouth were contending with. For clubs like Millwall, the sort who have spent most of their history in the middle two divisions, eight-figure debts are totally unprecedented, obligations out of all proportion to their financial potential. But while current trends in football continue, the only likelihood is that enormous debts of this variety will be revealed rather more frequently and that clubs' chances of escaping them will become rather smaller.

If this is true then the whole rationale behind the Premiership, the whole ostensible purpose of commercialisation, is no more than a rather bad joke at the expense of football. Because the whole idea was that football, in the bad old days, was moribund. Was debt-ridden. Was terminally strapped for cash. Was unable to generate a decent profit, and therefore (as if we cared) was unable to attract investors. And so it was, but the striking thing is not how desperate the problems were in football 15 years ago, but how trivial they seem, how slight, compared to those that clubs are facing now and those they will be facing in the future.

In 1981, when Oxford United thought they were going bust, their overdraft stood at around £175,000. This was a situation serious enough to cause the bank to stop honouring Oxford's cheques, yet it amounted to less than five per cent of the debt accumulated by Bournemouth, when *their* bank tried to have them closed in 1997. The comparison is pitiful. Increases in inflation, even taking into account the higher rate of inflation that has applied in football, cannot even come close to bridging the gap.

Chelsea's long-standing financial crisis resulted in them spending most of the Seventies and Eighties in mediocrity. They too brushed with closure. Meetings of creditors were held. Eventually, around the time of Ken Bates' takeover in 1982, their debts reached a massive total of three million pounds. In comparison, even given Chelsea's greater depth of support, Oxford's problems were small. But set against the sort of deficits that football clubs are dealing with today, three million pounds was comparative luxury.

Bournemouth and Millwall are far from being the most indebted clubs in football. Nottingham Forest, during the wrangling before their takeover, were revealed to be carrying debts of close to £15 million. Manchester City, undergoing convulsions of their own, were around £25 million in the red. These are not small clubs, and both can generate a lot of income. But it is difficult to see where they are going to find the money to make up that sort of shortfall.

The more you are in debt, the more that interest payments (at Maine Road, over a million pounds a year) swallow up a large proportion of your income, pushing you even further into the pit. Clubs can borrow money from rich supporters, but sugar-daddies, just as much as banks, want to be paid back eventually. All this on top of the need to chase the sort of expensive players who will bring back the crowds, a strategy which risks pushing up debts to even more insuperable levels.

Not much has changed. The problems of football clubs look very much like they always did, except that they loom larger. The solutions

73

they are looking for also look much the same. The Nineties do not always look all that different to the Eighties. Even some of the characters are the same. Tottenham fans, remembering the £18 million debt that made their club's situation so desperate some years ago, that they even looked to Robert Maxwell to help them out, will have been surprised to see Irving Scholar, whose leadership brought about that crisis, popping up at Forest as the brains behind the takeover. Sometimes it is hard to feel that football learns from its mistakes.

Scholar's main blunder at Tottenham was the purchase of a sportswear company called Hummel, which went under with massive debts that Tottenham were forced to take on. Millwall purchased a pub chain called Tavern Leisure for ten million pounds and sold it one year later for less than three million pounds. Diversification was the panacea then, and seems to be the panacea now. (As well as stock market flotation, of course, which contributed as much to Tottenham's crisis of 1991 as it did to Millwall's of 1997.) There are more clubs flirting with business ventures now than there were when Tottenham got their fingers burned. Walsall use the Bescot Stadium as a market. Fulham, for years, have been trying to rebuild Craven Cottage to incorporate luxury flats.

There are many other examples. There are a lot of schemes about. Some will work. Some will not. None of them are necessarily mistakes. But nor are they panaceas, and one suspects that some clubs who diversify do so out of desperation, hoping for a miracle cure, encouraged to leap before they look by the twin pressures of current debt and potential gain. The more that is the case, the more likely it is that many of these schemes will fail. The same is true of stadium construction. Practically every professional club in Britain has undertaken costly rebuilding or relocation work. This is usually thought of as a symptom of the game's financial health. But neither the Football Trust (whose budget has been devastated by the National Lottery), nor even the inevitable price rises are necessarily going to pay for all this work. Chelsea's financial crisis was caused by the construction of the East Stand. A similar fate may be in store for some of the more ambitious and more unlucky clubs.

Already one thinks of Millwall, whose move to the New Den was just as central to their crisis as their purchase of the pub chain. Oxford's experience is equally instructive. They bought a site and started building a new ground, but ran out of money halfway through and found themselves left with a half-finished stadium on a deserted building site. The resulting financial problems had very little in common with the rosy future which the club had promised the new development would bring.

Chelsea's misfortune was to build their new stand in the expectation, fuelled by increased public interest after 1966, that crowds were going to increase. They fell drastically. The current construction boom is similarly based on a boom in attendances and the assumption that that boom will carry on. While the boom continues, it will protect the game, for some time yet, from the consequences of debt. If crowds continue to rise, and gate receipts rise even faster, the apparent prosperity will convince a lot of people, particularly the investors. The banks will not feel the inclination to pull the plug. Expensive players and expensive stands will provide a feeling of optimism that will override most fans' concerns about the solidity of the foundations on which this spending may be based.

Indeed, the very fact of record debts may paradoxically look like evidence of financial health. If Manchester City can shrug off a debt nearly ten times that which nearly did for Chelsea in the early Eighties, it will be taken to prove how solid football's foundations have become. Perhaps the mountain of debt is nothing to be scared of. All prosperity is dependent on investment, and investment is dependent on willingness to incur a temporary debt. If Blackburn are prepared to lose ten million pounds a season, if Newcastle can lose twice that amount, what has football to be scared of? The system is expanding and provided it continues to expand the chickens need never come to roost.

If that was true we would be worrying for nothing. But whether it be house prices in the Eighties, or football in the Nineties, a boom is always followed by a bust. Nothing in the nature of football exempts it from this rule. The system will not expand for ever. Even if football remains in fashion, and fashion, by definition, is a passing thing, it cannot expand its audience indefinitely. It must reach a limit eventually, like an Albanian pyramid investment scheme. When it does, the crisis of confidence will follow.

This has already happened once at least in football, when the transfer market soared in the late Seventies, then crashed. Names like Kevin Reeves and Steve Daley play much the same part in the economic history of football as do Polly Peck and Maxwell in the collapse of the Lawson boom. The boom itself was what caused the bust. The greater the boom, the more that clubs will be confident to build up the very debts that will come back to crush them. The more the boom produces money for clubs to spend, the more it creates the expectation of returns on that spending, the more that even clubs with greater caution are forced to join in or fall behind the high-spenders. You can only stretch elastic so far. Eventually it springs back and hits you in the face.

Football does not need to collapse, to find its stands deserted, before it finds its economic fortunes going into reverse. It only requires that previous expectations of prosperity turn out to be exaggerated, so that previous investment decisions prove to have been unwise. How long before the boom is exposed as a bubble? It may indeed be pay-per-view which brings the crash about, decimating the television income of clubs whose flotations, and spending, have been based on high expectations and high income from the Premiership deal. Perhaps one or two clubs may crash for other reasons, and thereby shake the market's confidence in the sector as a whole. At that point, the greater the confidence the market had before, the more money has been extended to the game as a result, the greater will be the panic and the swifter the fall.

There is a limited extent to which clubs like Middlesbrough, or Coventry, can go on spending millions for the pleasure of flirting with, or suffering, relegation. There is a limited extent to which a club like Bournemouth can go on heaping up losses before it can do so no longer. There is a limited extent to which a club like Oxford can get away with engaging in expensive projects and making a mess of them. The outlines of a future crash are always visible in the circumstances of the present. If not these particular clubs, then others are not going to make it.

There is no reason why any professional club should close. All of them have the potential to survive for another one hundred years or more if they get the chance. But some are bound to be so choked by debt, so weighed down by interest, that if they are larger clubs, they will fall into obscurity, or, if they are smaller clubs, they will quite likely close. When they do, the culprits will be those who revelled in the Nineties boom, who were convinced, as people are during any period of prosperity, that it would never come to an end. It can, it will, and the victims will not be those who have made the money from the boom, but those supporters who have paid most of the money to sustain it.

10. A DISTORTED PICTURE

Everything that is wrong with football can be blamed on television. Nearly everything that is wrong with football *should* be blamed on television. It runs football, so it can take the blame. It is more powerful, within the game, than anything or anybody from the game itself. Whatever happens in the game, whatever happens to the game, happens either (however indirectly) because of television's influence, or directly, because television says so. It has enormous power and it mostly uses it for ill. This is true of Rupert Murdoch's empire. But it is true also of both the BBC and ITV.

This is so because much of the money which has destabilised the game has come from television. It is television which has hyped football to the point of saturation. It is the profit which television promises which causes the financial whirligig to spin. It is the way in which television chooses to distribute its wealth which has caused the game to strain and split.

The most crucial thing to understand about the financial contribution of television is that it is divided very differently from the contribution of the paying supporter. It inflates vastly the income of the largest clubs in relation to the income of the smaller clubs. Television is the medium of the casual fan, the less attached, and therefore is wildly skewed towards the top end of the market, famous clubs, famous players, the show and the spectacle rather than the local and provincial. It therefore changes utterly the financial balance of the game.

The pot divides up differently according to which clubs appear on television most often and which clubs are shown in the FA Cup and

Europe. But the current Sky deal with the Premiership means that each club in the Premiership should receive around eight million pounds a season for their trouble. Meanwhile, Sky's agreement with the League allows each First Division Club to make something like half a million pounds. (Each Second and Third Division club makes just about enough to buy a satellite system for the social club and maybe a subscription to the Disney channel.) That is a difference between the average in the Premiership and the average in Division One of something in the region of 16 to one.

That is out of all proportion to their respective levels of support. Attendances in the Premiership are only about twice what they are in Division One. Allow for higher ticket prices and Premiership receipts might be three times higher than those in Division One. Let us say four times, to be generous. Compared to 16 times the television income, those differentials are nothing. As for some clubs the income for television may actually exceed their income through the turnstiles, the impact of television in distorting the market is more than appreciable.

The choices made by television are unbalanced in relation to the choices that supporters make. But they are also unbalanced in relation to the choices television viewers make. Wherever possible, television selects its games on a winner-takes-all principle. Given a game that might attract eight million viewers and one that might attract only six million, they won't select proportionately, picking the first game four times out of seven and the other game for the other three. They'll pick the same game seven times in a row. It is as if the BBC were to show nothing but *EastEnders*, on the grounds that it had the highest viewing figures and should therefore be shown all the time.

When Chelsea beat Middlesbrough to win the FA Cup, it was the fourth time, of a possible six, that the BBC had televised a tie involving Chelsea, and the first time that they had not had the opportunity of showing someone else. Sixty-four teams competed in the last six rounds of the FA Cup, but as far as the BBC were concerned there was only one club competing. Lucky for them, they picked the winners. But in doing so they did no favours to the game or, ultimately, to themselves.

This was a year in which the FA Cup produced, by common consent, its most diverse and interesting competition for years. The Big Five (whether you include Newcastle or Everton among their number) were all eliminated before the last 16. The whole appeal of the FA Cup rests on its mixture of clubs of all abilities and sizes. That is its heritage. It was a heritage the BBC ignored completely, eschewing diversity for the sake

78

of the largest possible audience share. It was beyond them to select a tie involving any club outside the Premiership. This was not the first time that the BBC has failed to understand, or care about, the nature of the competition they have bought. In previous years Liverpool were granted a monopoly position, in others Manchester United, and then Chelsea – at the very time when the FA Cup defied the economic trends in football which threaten to render it so dull.

The whole existence of a licence-funded station depends on the presumption that there is more to broadcasting than a short-term dash for audience share. Minority interests and a long-term view are crucial to that understanding. Similarly, the whole existence of the FA Cup, and that of football as a cultural institution rather than a vehicle for producing profit, depends on the presumption that diversity should be encouraged. If the BBC behaves like Rupert Murdoch, interested at all times only in the largest market share, it attacks the principles which sustain it as well as reducing the greatest sporting competition in the world to a mere replay of the Premiership. There are people in the BBC who realise this and regret it, but say that in market conditions they have no choice. But all that proves is that television, in the marketplace, is no real friend to football.

Television will try to mould football into whatever shape it chooses. We have not yet been subjected to the sort of pressure Rupert Murdoch put on rugby league. Apart from moving it around the calendar and trying to enforce mergers on unwilling clubs, Sky TV decided that Keighley, champions of Division Two the previous season, should not be promoted because they would not attract a sufficient television audience. No stunt like that has yet been pulled in football. But it would hardly be beyond the television stations.

Football may be bigger, more powerful and even further steeped in tradition than rugby league, yet on the other hand the potential profits are much greater. If anything, television may try to go even further than it has in rugby league. If it does, if television brings the same logic to football as kept Keighley out of Super League, then we are on the fast track to a franchise system.

Television already makes all the important decisions in football. The major competitions have been reinvented to suit its requirements. The First Division became the Premiership at television's urging. The European Cup became the Champions' League, initially excluding some nations' champions on the blatant yet unspoken basis that they were not what the major European television stations wanted. Television already tries to select its own competitors. How long before the Barnsleys and the Wimbledons are kept out of a showcase competition because they are not the sort of attraction that television wants?

Television already thinks that its word is law. Its word does indeed seem to be the law. For some years now the views and interests of supporters have been of no consequence in deciding when matches shall kick-off or whether the dates for which they are arranged shall change. We have become accustomed to a Sunday kick-off at one o'clock, killing your chance to have a drink before the match, to compulsory kick-offs on a Friday evening, to a regular Thursday date for the Rangers-Celtic match. Games are rearranged at a few days' notice, kick-offs brought forward to noon or put back to the evening regardless of the problems caused for travelling supporters. The sole consideration is the convenience of television.

This need not even mean the convenience of people watching on the box at home. The 1994 League Cup final was put back to a bizarre kick-off time, five o'clock, so that ITV could curry favour with rugby union by showing the Hong Kong Sevens, and thereby help its bid for coverage of rugby's World Cup. It is not clear what benefits football gained by allowing ITV to do this. It is clear that the enhanced prestige of the League Cup final was not among them.

Referees now delay the second half until they are permitted, by a signal from the touchline, to restart the game because the advertising break has finished. This may not matter very much in principle but it does go to illustrate what football really means to television. We are squeezed in between the adverts and we are there to make the TV channels more attractive for the advertisers.

Television does not take football seriously. It has bought the game but wants only that part of it which is most profitable and most shallow. Of course there are many minor exceptions to this rule, an increasing number of documentaries about police violence against supporters, about ticket touting, about black players of the past and present, and about many other subjects, but they tend to be restricted to the minority channels. Mainstream programming mostly shuns these topics. Its idea of a frank discussion of the issues is to debate whether Robbie Fowler is better than Les Ferdinand.

Television shows very little interest in the economics of the game. The problems at Millwall and at Bournemouth, stories breaking in the press in the same week, both went unmentioned on the following Saturday's *Football Focus*. You would search the major channels practically in vain for the debate over all-seater stadia, for any mention of the plight of the priced-out supporter. Subjects like these go far closer to the roots, and future, of the game than do the trivial talking points that pass for television's agenda. Are serious issues in football of little interest to supporters? The plethora of fanzines would seem to give the lie to any such suggestion. But television chooses to think otherwise. It is tempting to speculate whether it is always keen to see criticised a game which makes it so much money, and to whose problems it has itself contributed so much.

Even at a time when supporters' views are becoming more widely read, when fanzines have changed the way that football is reported, fans are still very far from the centre of the game as it is seen on television. We are little more than noises off, never able to express our opinions at any length, rarely closer to the microphone than a position in the audience. Comment is restricted to the professionals or veterans, to those who constitute the game as television sees it. The only possible conclusion is that fans are considered to lie outside the game, or at best, around its edges. There is no space on television for the view that fans are at the very centre of the game.

Therefore television coverage, no matter how extensive it becomes, is mostly trivial, mostly inadequate, mostly and especially irritating. The 'whoosh' sound that accompanies the action replays on Sky TV. The inability of Don Howe or Kevin Keegan to communicate so much as one per cent of what they understand about the game in return for their sizeable retainers as celebrity summarisers. The sycophancy of Bob Wilson and Brian Moore. The assumption of the pundits that their viewers must be supporting Manchester United and Rangers in the Champions' League. A taste for gimmickry, a fundamental lack of contact with the world of supporters, an inability to separate people's reputations from their understanding of the needs of an audience. Things like these tell supporters that television controls football but is uncomfortable with it, that it is nervous of the passions and criticisms of supporters, that it would rather trivialise than genuinely popularise the game.

Television fails football several times over. It fails football by not respecting its traditions. It fails football by destroying its economic balance. It fails football by ignoring the supporters. Yet it need not do any of these. As a potential populariser of the game, television has no equal. It could do us so much good. It does do us a lot of good. It is just that it does not make up for the damage that it does.

Television brings people to football. There can be few who come to British football grounds without having seen the game on television first. That has been true for 20 years and more. Television makes supporters.

It was once feared that having too much football on television would cause attendances to plummet. It has not happened. There *is* too much football on television, but for every fan who has become a couch potato, there may be two new fans who have been brought to football by discovering it on television. Ticket prices keep people at home. (Supporters priced out of the élite clubs may have no reason to thank television for attracting thousands of casual supporters to their grounds.) But in itself television coverage does not.

In fact television is almost solely responsible for the boom in football, for the rising attendances. It is not the Premiership, not the foreign stars, not the all-seaters which have brought supporters back, but, basically, the saturation coverage of football. It is not just the televising of live matches, or even the highlights packages, but the constant reference to football, in trailers, in previews, in advertising. Football, which used to skulk at the fag-end of the schedule, is now impossible to get away from. The difference is so great as to be practically immeasurable. It is all free advertising for football and its effect could only be to bring about an increase in the public's interest in football proportionate to the increase in football's visibility.

Overwhelmingly, this advertising is centred on the Premiership and it is, therefore, the Premiership which is the major beneficiary. It need not be that way. Put Dulwich Hamlet or Leek Town on satellite television every night and their crowds would go up as well.

The élite clubs may be the beneficiaries of saturation coverage, but even so, for the first time, we can see live Second and Third Division games on television. It increases interest and awareness, makes the names of local heroes better known than they have been for years, possibly since the demise of the local sporting press and the rise of national television. News programmes enable people to watch their local players every week. Until their relegation to the Conference, I could see more of Hereford United, on my local news, than I might have seen, 20 years ago of some teams in the old First Division.

That familiarity has not bred contempt. At the same time as television has allowed the economic devastation of the lower divisions, it has enabled people to understand the real value of what is being destroyed. That is the nature of television, torn between the marketplace and the social arena, between the safe and the imaginative, the dumb and the informative. That's how it can give to us, just as it takes away. But the greater balance is on the side of the taking.

Television adopts the guise of a provider. But where it can, it prefers not to provide football but to withhold it, to restrict the audience, to opt for a smaller audience that can pay rather than a larger audience which can't. It is interesting that at a time when television channels have multiplied many times over, the supporters' complaint is that they have too little access to the game on television. The great majority of fans who do not have satellite TV actually see less live football on television, at home, than they could see ten years ago. The first Chesterfield–Middlesbrough semi-final might have been one of the most exciting games that I had ever seen. As it was, it was one of the most exciting games that I have ever *heard.* I had to 'watch it' as it were, on the radio. International matches which the BBC would like to show disappear from terrestrial channels, except for Channel Five, who were allowed to buy the Poland–England match despite the fact that half the country couldn't pick it up. This is not a process of provision. It is a process of exclusion.

The next exclusionary step is going to be pay-per-view. This will be sold to us on the basis that we will be able to watch all our club's home games. This we can do now if we are the holder of a season ticket. What we can also do now is watch, occasionally, other clubs on television. Some of these would like to prevent us, particularly the largest – whom we may already not be able to afford to watch live.

Consider the ethical nature of this process. Money is concentrated in the hands of a very few clubs, with the justification that as this enables them to buy the best players in Europe, it will enable us to watch the best in Europe. The immediate outcome was that we were unable to afford to see these players performing live. That was not good enough. The next step is to prevent us seeing them on television either.

There is going to be no apology for this, only the greed and arrogance of men who have made much money but feel they are being prevented by bureaucracy from making quite as much as they would like. David Murray lays into the scroungers: 'Rangers played Aberdeen in a stadium worth £60 million and with £30 million worth of players on the park, and the general public could just switch on for nothing. That's not on.' How hard a time David Murray has had of it, laying on Ibrox Park and Glasgow Rangers at personal expense for the entertainment, free and gratis, of the public. It may not appear to be free to the advertisers who pay for the TV channels, to the TV channels that are paying for the match, to the public who pay licence fees to watch the television. But evidently David Murray and his fellow chairmen feel it's them who are being ripped off, and they are not prepared to stand for it. So pay-per-view is coming whether it is convenient for fans or not.

How much is it going to cost to watch the élite clubs on pay-per-view?

Most estimates start at upwards of £200 a season. But for most of us, the answer is not one single penny. Many supporters are not prepared to be ripped off quite as much as that. That is the Murdochisation of football. That is what television and the market are doing to us. They offer us everything and leave us with nothing. Pay-per-view is the ultimate combination of the two.

What has television done for football fans? Very soon we are going to have to pay rather more to watch some teams on television than, ten years ago, we paid to watch them live. That is a scandal and an insult. If that is television's contribution to the game then we would have been better off without it. Originally, supporters were at the game and television wasn't. Then television was at the game – and then, supporters could not afford to be. Now television will be at the game and supporters will not even be able to watch it on the television. We can indeed blame television for most of what is wrong with football. That blame is not misplaced.

11. THE DAY THE GAME WAS SOLD

It was television which brought about the Premiership. Therefore it was television which finally sold us out. If we wanted football not to be dedicated to the fleecing of its customers, if we didn't want the production of endless, empty hype, if we wanted football to resist the domination of television and its demands, then the moment when the Premiership was created was probably the last chance to abort the process and prevent the game spinning entirely beyond control.

The Premiership is nothing more than a cartel for monopolising income. Without it, the financial frenzy could not have taken off. Once the Premiership came into being, that frenzy could not be stopped. The Premiership is the enemy of football. Not necessarily the clubs that play in it, and not at all the people who follow those football clubs, and are, as a result, ripped off or replaced. The Premiership is not the enemy because it is the top division. Far from it. The old First Division was something which other clubs, and supporters, regarded with respect. It contained most of the best teams and most of the best players. It stood at the summit of the game. Yet it wasn't trying to obscure, let alone close down, the rest of football. The enemy is the breakaway, the quasi-independent league, the Premiership as a separate entity, lording it over all the rest of football.

You cannot speak of the interests of football as a whole and then have a separate Premiership. The whole reason the Premiership is separate is so that it can take decisions without reference to the rest of football. It was the Premiership which decided to break away, which decided that the rest of football was its enemy, which decided it could only prosper

85

over the prostrate body of the rest of football. It follows that the rest of football, including the supporters, could only prosper over the dead body of the Premiership.

The Premiership has been in place for little more than half a decade. In football terms, in terms of football's traditions, it is new. Yet it is the Premiership which is treated as an institution, the rest of football which is assumed to be impermanent. The structure of the Football League is regularly called into question. All sorts of ill-judged proposals are made for feeder teams, regional divisions and part-time football, all of which are nothing more than quick fixes whose effects would be to make worse the problems they are designed to solve. The real problem is never addressed, since the problem is the huge increase in inequalities of income. The cause of that is the Premiership. Nothing in football is sacred, except the one thing that shouldn't be.

Yet there is no reason, no sporting reason, for the Premiership to exist. There is no reason for anything other than a top division, of a pyramidal structure, linking the lowest with the highest clubs. We didn't need it, nor did we ask for it. There was no public demand for it to split from the body of the League. Nor was there any reason to allow the split to happen. There was the pusillanimous excuse that if they were not permitted to set up the Premiership, the rich club owners would have broken away of their own accord. It is the most obscure of arguments which claims that if you give people everything they ask for in advance, you stop them getting everything they want. You might as well claim you could save your job by handing in your notice.

The emergence of the Premiership was not inevitable. Attempts at a breakaway *were* inevitable, but their success was not. Previous forays had been beaten back. Irving Scholar, always the first to come up with a bad idea, was talking about it as early as 1982. Philip Carter, when he was supposed to be negotiating a television deal on behalf of the whole League in 1988, attempted to do a deal instead on behalf on the so-called 'Big Ten' clubs, including his club, Everton. The result was a public furore. Bobby Charlton was so angry that he stood for office in opposition, protesting: 'If I get on the management committee I'll fight like hell to maintain the Third and Fourth Divisions. I'm not interested in having a Super League. Our League is 92 clubs, and that's why it's the best.' Fine words, particularly coming from a director of Manchester United. Charlton's philosophy may be a little different from that which now prevails at Old Trafford. But it was, nevertheless, a philosophy that prevailed at the time. Carter and his friends were reviled, outvoted and kicked out. What was possible in 1988 should have been possible in

1991. Instead, the great body of football clubs (if any group as spineless as a collection of club chairmen can be described as a *body*) was bullied into signing its own death warrant.

It was the easiest of victories, and the most triumphant. No sooner had the League handed power to the Premiership than the Premiership had assumed a totally dominant position in the game. The Premiership aimed to monopolise as much of football's income as it could. To do so it needed to monopolise the attention of the public. To do that, it needed to monopolise the attention of the media. By and large, it has done so. To many people, the Premiership *is* football. It is almost the only football that they ever hear about, or read about. Most of the broadsheets, as much as the tabloids, have joined in the adoration.

They compete to see who can produce the largest section devoted to the Premiership. Crosstables of matches played so far, dates of outstanding games, all sorts of superfluous statistics, even diagrams depicting the formations of all 20 sides, as if we came into work on Monday and talked each other through the tactics of the 20 different managers in the Premiership. The rest of football is squeezed into an overcrowded space somewhere at the bottom, with truncated tables and results in smaller print, with match reports that are noticeable by their absence. The Football League descends to the level of an afterthought. Sometimes it appears not to exist at all. The phrase *the football season* has disappeared and *the Premiership season* has taken its place. The Premiership is all there is.

News programmes, which used to give all the results, prefer now to report only the Premiership scores. Steve Rider rushes through League scores on the teleprinter, as if fearing he would offend his audience if he took his time and read them properly. The only conclusion anyone could draw is that unless a game is being played in the Premiership, it isn't worth reading about, thinking about or talking about. Football outside the Premiership is second-rate. Casual followers are amazed when First and Second Division sides, as they do regularly, knock sides from the Premiership out of the cups. They have been led to believe that the Premiership is stuffed with talent, while teams outside it are little better than triers, scufflers and no-hopers. Otherwise, why would the media devote so little time to reporting their games? The Premiership could scarcely do a better job on its own behalf if it actually owned the newspapers.

Sports editors apparently assume that people who follow football are only interested in the Premiership. We are not. In fact, only about half of all paying spectators watch the Premiership. Less than half, if we include people who watch non-league football. Over any given weekend about half a million people will watch professional football matches in England and Wales, and about a quarter of a million will watch the League, about the same number as watch the Premiership. Most of the highest crowds will be in the Premiership, but by no means all. On a good weekend the top two Third Division attendances might equal one of the lower attendances in the Premiership. This ratio of interest is simply not reflected in the way newspapers cover football.

Of course most of the supporters who watch the League are watching not because they think it's better than the Premiership, but because they're mostly interested in whatever game their team is playing in. Which only goes to show that supporters are primarily interested in the personal involvement, rather than the spectacle. Most journalists appear to think that the Premiership is about *mouthwatering prospects*, but in the League they find the *quality disappointing*. That is not the way we look at it. Quality matters, but it is not the only thing, or the most important. If the football pages reflected the way real supporters watch real football, they would look very different.

The football pages are more boring, not more glamorous, as a result of their obsession with the Premiership. That is entirely appropriate, the Premiership being the most boring, because the most unequal, of the four professional divisions. It is uncompetitive in the extreme. It is probably easier to predict the top three in the Premiership than to predict the winners of Division Two or Three. The essence of sport is a true competition. The Premiership does not provide such a competition. It is designed to prevent competition taking place. Yet our interest in the game is supposed to centre on the 'race for the Premiership', a race which, for most of the contestants, never starts.

Yet the media persist in finding the Premiership more interesting than it really is. They seem to be dazzled by the image it projects. When it is not manufacturing money, the Premiership is manufacturing myths. It is particularly keen on promoting the myth of improving playing standards. It may be in the interests of the football industry to talk up the successes of the Premiership, but it is in the interests of supporters to tell the truth, and that truth is that the Emperor's new clothes exist mostly in his imagination.

There is a lot of wishful thinking going on as far as playing standards are concerned. The presence of many overseas players in the Premiership is at the core of the argument. But the first question that comes to mind is: to whose standards are we referring? Given the growing inequality *within* the Premiership, something which scarcely anyone denies, are we talking about the top of the Premiership or the bottom?

If the bottom, then, are the overseas players really better than the domestic players who preceded them, or those who play alongside them still? Juninho was, at Middlesbrough. Others have had some successes. It is no more than a truism to observe that some overseas players have done well, others not. Some have been superb. Others have been prestige signings, trophy signings, good for the sale of shirts, for the profile and the reputation of a club. But others are simply Bosman signings, made either because their wage levels are still below British levels, or because transfer fees, which remained payable for domestic players out-of-contract, did not remain so for players from overseas. One thinks of Graeme Souness' transfer policy. He stuffed Southampton full of overseas players, and not a household name among them. He kept them up, but that didn't mean Southampton were a better team than they used to be.

These Bosman signings are no better and no worse than the domestic players whom these clubs would have signed in previous years. It is not that standards are rising but that goalposts, in the transfer market, have been moved. There are, of course, a handful of clubs who have gained access to the pool of world-class players through the money that the Premiership has generated for them. These clubs would previously have had their pick of domestic talent. Now they have the opportunity to shop abroad as well. Zola, Asprilla, Bergkamp. Without doubt there are more players of this class playing in this country than there were before. The numbers should not be exaggerated. We are talking about a handful. Nor should the benefits to supporters be exaggerated. We could see Gianfranco Zola almost as easily on television when he was in Italy as we can now that he is playing in England.

Nor are the clubs they play for necessarily producing better football teams than they did in the past. As they cannot be directly matched against each other, there is no better, no alternative yardstick than to measure the performance of the Premiership in Europe, against that of their predecessors in the old First Division. By 1997, after five seasons, no Premiership club had yet won any competition other than Arsenal winning the Cup Winners' Cup. None had reached the final of the European Cup, or the UEFA Cup. This must be balanced against the fact that from 1965 to 1982, there was an English finalist in a European competition every single season.

Eighteen consecutive seasons. Perhaps the standard of competition may have risen since. And the Heysel ban deprived English clubs of

European experience. But they have been back a long time now. Several have had more experience than had a number of English clubs that won European trophies in the past. This evidence does not support the proposition of a rise in standards in the Premiership.

The major improvement among Premiership players has been in the standard of remuneration they receive for being no better than their forebears in the old First Division. Their wages have leapt far ahead, both of those on offer in the recent past, and of those on offer in the current First Division. Differentials are such that almost no club in the First Division can afford to keep a player who is wanted in the Premiership. They try to keep up. Higher wages in the Premiership successfully exert a pressure for higher wages in the First Division. But the gap is quite impossible for most clubs to bridge.

Yet this does not mean that the difference in standards between those divisions has widened in the same way wage differentials have. People do not become better players just because it becomes possible to pay them more. Wage differentials are not proportionate to differences in ability. A player who, by the smallest sliver, fails to impress a Premiership club enough to sign him on, may be paid only a third as much as a very slightly better player who makes it to the Premiership. The gap grows but the difference in ability does not. Small differences in ability are marked by enormous disparities in income. This principle should not come as a surprise to anyone who has lived in Britain for the last 20 years.

The image is one of a 'growing gap' in football – the phrase crops up again and again – between the Premiership and the League, between the top 20 and the rest. Yet the Cup upsets still continue as they did before. Clubs relegated from the Premiership, despite their financial advantages, do not necessarily find themselves crushing all opposition. For every Bolton there is a Norwich or a QPR, finding life harder than their preconceptions led them to expect. Promoted clubs are not automatically relegated. Perhaps they are more likely to struggle than they were. But then again, the Premiership is smaller than the old First Division, so that between the contenders for Europe and the relegation-threatened, there is no real middle ground.

Too many lazy assumptions are made, accepting the picture of a rich Premiership, packed with stars, and a dull, penurious League falling ever further behind. Yet we are mostly talking about the same sort, the same standard of players as were playing before the Premiership caused them to be hyped beyond their true ability. One might even argue that the First Division is better than the old Second Division, simply because some clubs are not finding it possible to sell their best players. The transfer income of First Division clubs has slumped. Good players who, in the past, would have played at the top level, are now competing with the Bosman signings. It is harder to move up, so some clubs keep their best players for longer and play a better standard of football as a result.

This doesn't mean that money doesn't buy you anything in football. Of course it does. Blackburn, or Newcastle, or Chelsea, did not build better sides without having millions to make it easier. Nor does it mean that a gap is not opening up in football. There is. But it doesn't mean that the distance, at any given time, between the fifth-placed team and the 16th, or between the 16th and the 30th, is any greater than it ever was. Why should it be?

It means that the 30th can no longer seriously aspire to be fifth, that the 16th can rise occasionally to fifth but not aspire to stay there. And it is a difference not between the Premiership and the First Division, but between the élite of the Premiership and everybody else.

Where are the Stokes, the Ipswiches, the QPRs, the Watfords, the sort of clubs that spent several years, in the Seventies and Eighties, seriously competing, if not for the title, then for top six places? The answer is that today they have to sell their players before they get anywhere near that level. Good *teams* are emerging all the time and always will, but today, because of the enormous difference between what provincial clubs can pay and what the élite have to offer, none but the élite can keep a side together. The best of the provincial bunch were always able to keep a core of players and, in that way, keep up with their big-city rivals. They can no longer.

Nor can they keep their managers. The miracles that Brian Clough worked at Derby and at Forest would be most unlikely now. An élite club might offer to quadruple the wages of a contemporary Clough as an incentive to leave his old club in the lurch. More than one promoted club has been ripped apart at the moment of promotion by losing a manager. Both Bolton, after Bruce Rioch, and Swindon, after Glenn Hoddle, spent months floundering about and came bottom of the Premiership as a result.

Most clubs can no longer keep together a successful team. Without that ability it is hard to get to the top and almost impossible to stay there (a rule to which Wimbledon have been an exception). Conversely, for the élite clubs it is harder to fail, and far harder to slip towards the relegation zone, than it was before the Premiership. Future generations may find it impossible to believe that Tottenham and Manchester United were both relegated in the Seventies. You get too many chances to buy your way out of your mistakes. You have the chance to put too many internationals in the reserves to cover for the ones who fail. These clubs are no longer obliged to live with their mistakes. Aston Villa can shrug off Savo Milosevic.

So it is not that money guarantees success, but that without it, success is chimerical at best. And if money doesn't guarantee success, it does at least, as near as dammit, provide insurance against failure. Clubs like Liverpool and Manchester United may be no further ahead of the pack than they ever were, but from now on, it is *always* going to be Liverpool and Manchester United in front, and the pack will always be the pack. Money is going to freeze the game at one particular moment in time.

That will be a sterile future. You can bring over all the superstars you like, but no matter how many names you change, we are going to notice that the club names are always the same. Too much of the future is going to feel like it is being shoved, unwanted, down our throats. If anything it is going to get worse. The revolution is going to devour its own children. The Premiership has polarised the game between the haves and the have-nots, but that polarisation has affected the Premiership itself as much as anywhere. It is not hard to imagine further splits as the divergences in interest within the Premiership become ever more apparent, as the thieves fall out among themselves.

Because however permanent the Premiership seems to have become, by its own example it has shown how the game can be split up and reinvented at the convenience of television and the élite clubs. That, above all, is the reason why the breakaway should not have been permitted. Once you establish the precedent, it is far easier to get away with it a second time. If the Premiership doesn't prove a convenient vehicle for the interests of the rich, they can find a new one and throw the Premiership away.

The Premiership, so smug now and so arrogant, may be no more than a stepping-stone towards something even worse. After all, is the Premiership really the showcase that the television companies wanted? When their secret negotiations were in progress, it was the Big Ten, not the Slightly Smaller Twenty, whom the television companies wanted. The Premiership was a compromise, a political convenience, a body of clubs large enough to engineer a breakaway, rather than the ideal breakaway as such. Many of the clubs who play in it are of no real interest to the television companies.

It is a matter of potential audience. Television wants to show games that have the largest audience possible across the country. Therefore they want to show those clubs whose appeal is national, or near-national, rather than local. Tottenham's casual support is spread across the entire south of England. Liverpool's covers the country as a whole. Compared to these clubs, Bolton or Coventry or Sheffield Wednesday have nothing to offer. Television begrudges the millions it pays them. Quite possibly, maybe through the intervention of pay-per-view, a way will be found to throw the provincial clubs overboard, just as the smaller League clubs were previously disposed of.

The cracks have begun to show already in disputes over fixture pile-ups and the future of the League Cup. The size of the Premiership is coming under scrutiny in anticipation of the European League, and that may very well provide the opportunity for another split. Rick Parry left the Premiership for a job with Liverpool. Perhaps Parry, who knows better than anyone what is happening at the centre of the game, has seen which way the wind is blowing.

In some ways it matters very little. Perhaps the Premiership will be around for decades, or perhaps its days are numbered. The pass has already been sold. Once the Premiership was allowed to make the rules, it was already laid down that we were no longer interested in the greatest good of the greatest number. It is no use anyone complaining now about the greed and selfishness it has let loose. What else did anybody think it was going to be about?

The Premiership has swept through football like a forest fire. A lot of those who helped to light it have noticed that they're getting burned. Its successes are mostly mythological. Its drawbacks are increasingly evident. Its exploitation of supporters is entirely real. The foundation of the Premiership was the moment when the game was sold for good. It doesn't look like we are ever going to get it back.

12. COMPARISONS ARE ODIOUS

What they want to do is throw away the cake and keep the icing. They want the glamour but they do not want the game. The two are set against each other, the élite clubs against the body of the game, and such are the competitive economics of the game that every time we spend our money on the former, the latter falls even further behind. But this isn't what we want. The two compete when they should be mutually supportive.

It should never be the function, or the intention, of the richest section of the game to make it harder for the rest of football to survive. Why should Manchester United or Tottenham Hotspur want to make it harder for Rochdale or Exeter to stay in business? Rochdale and Exeter aren't trying to put Tottenham and Manchester United out of business. They cannot damage them. In no real sense are they even trying to compete with them. They want to play the élite in the cups. They want to aspire to play at the same level as them, even though they will probably never get there. They are not offering either the same kind of football or the same kind of experience of football, that the élite do. Yet many thousands of people watch, enjoy and appreciate football clubs like these. You cannot write these clubs off as unwanted.

But the rich clubs drive out the smaller ones. They drive them out economically. They drive them out of public view. The lower divisions are so often assumed to be of little importance, as if they were simply third-rate, inferior versions of the sort of clubs who compete for the Premiership, as if they had nothing to recommend them, as if there were nothing intrinsically interesting about them, as if we would lose nothing by getting rid of them. As if the people who watched this football were getting something fundamentally inferior, as if they were doomed to have a dull and miserable time watching dull and miserable football, football outside the charmed circle of the Liverpools and Arsenals.

Football is not like that. Watching the game as played outside the élite few, or in the lower divisions, or in the Conference, or in the leagues below, is not a fundamentally inferior way of appreciating football. It is, in some ways, fundamentally different. But that is among football's many pleasures. It represents many varied worlds within a single game. There should be room for all of them.

Fever Pitch is as good a guide as any. One of the most interesting things about that book, a book which is generally about watching Arsenal in the top half of the top division, is that it does not confine itself only to Arsenal. It ranges from Highbury to Kenilworth Road, the Abbey Stadium, Saffron Walden, school football and casual football with friends. One reason so many fans liked *Fever Pitch* was that it said so many things we understood instinctively. Among these, it understood that although football forms a hierarchy in which a pyramid of leagues establishes exactly who stands where, it is not a hierarchy of enjoyment. It's not as if there were the best of football, exhilarating, at the top and then, beneath it, inferior, unsatisfying football, something we merely tolerate for want of something better. That is not what football is about at all.

There must be room for all and an understanding of all. Football games need to be understood, and reported, in the context of what they are actually about, what are the supporters' expectations, what the people who go to watch expect to see. If Gillingham play Southend at Priestfield, nobody expects to see a troupe of internationals. Nobody goes there by accident, imagining they are going to see the sort of game they might see if Ajax were playing Juventus, and then walks out disgusted because they are not. Of course everybody wants to see the players produce the best standard of football and the best game that they can. We hope to see some good football and to see a good game. And the chances are we will. But there is no point in a journalist watching a game in the Second Division and comparing it unfavourably to the Premiership.

There are many reporters who cannot write about a lower division match, on the rare occasions that they are sent to them, without giving the impression that they resent their editor sending them to watch some provincial no-hopers from a draughty press box when they could be watching somebody glamorous in easy reach of the London Underground, writing about household names in comfort, getting home before the early editions come out. The lower divisions are not some miserable squalor-ridden outpost of lousy football watched by people who know no better. The clubs who play in them are not usually as good, *team against team*, as in the Premiership but *in their way*, a different way, the football they produce is not inferior.

A good game is still a good game no matter in what division it is played. A bitter struggle is a bitter struggle at any level. A tedious draw is no more enlightening in the Premiership than one played halfway up the Third Division. Certainly the thrilling moments of great skill, to which all supporters are attracted, are more plentiful the higher up the divisions that we go. But these moments are not absent from lower-division football. And they are not, on their own, what makes a great game of football.

Comparisons are odious. Nor are they always made without some application of a double standard. Liverpool have played several games of great excitement in recent years, often against Newcastle. Games finishing three-all, four-three, games that have the exaggerated tag of 'match of the decade' applied to them in the following morning's papers. These have been thrilling games but games which were made possible not just by skill but by mistakes, mistakes which if committed outside the Premiership would have led to adverse comment about the quality of the game on offer. These games were thrilling all right. But equally thrilling football can be seen at any level, thrilling not because of the talent on the pitch but because of the ebb and flow of the melodrama.

You have to want your club to play at a higher level. Football requires us to have that aspiration, or there *is* no melodrama. But I have seen Oxford play in three divisions and I would lie if I said that the football I saw was any more enjoyable, or any less agonising, in any one division than in any other.

We have a small élite of football clubs, in England and elsewhere, who are all growing to resemble one another, and this handful of clones, these distant and expensive clubs, are all the game is now supposed to be about. They are the showcase. They are supposed to show off everything that's best about the game. They are supposed to be the best. But what is *best*? What are the pleasures of football? What are those things we treasure most about the game?

It depends on whether you are, basically, a travelling supporter or a television viewer. Much of the game is lost to the television viewer. They miss out on so much. They see so little, feel so little, they understand so little. If all they see in football is that the most skilful players are better to watch than those who are less skilful, that may be because they have no opportunity to see what else there is on offer. So they may very well find it hard to understand why anyone might prefer Stockport to Manchester United, might choose to drive 200 miles to see Grimsby, might stand out on an open terrace in the rain to watch a Third Division club rather than turn on the television in the warm and dry and watch the famous names of Arsenal.

But for those who experience the game at closer quarters, what is this *best* for us? If any of us were to compile a list of what we cherished most about the game, of what stuck in the memory, of what we most appreciated, would we really list no more than a roll-call of internationals and of trophy winners? I might indeed have Alan Shearer on my list, and John Barnes, and Johann Cruyff, and John Aldridge, and any number of players of whom everyone has heard. But for as long as I remember any of these I'll remember a left-back called Mike Ford, of whom most people haven't heard but who is memorable for his passion and his rapport with the crowd. I'll remember Peter Lorimer not for any of the goals he scored, but for the day I saw him get sent off at Oxford, and I'll remember another striker, Billy Whitehurst, not because he was any good but because he wasn't.

I may remember John Hall, and Eric Hall, and Martin Edwards, but not, I think, with any pleasure. Alex Ferguson would make the list, but more for his arrogance than for his ability, and the images of Brian Clough that stay with me are less those of his footballers than those of his ravaged face. If I was thinking, now, of managers, I'd much more likely think of Martin O'Neill, or Dario Gradi, or of John Sitton, calling Leyton Orient supporters 'cockroaches' on television on the way to getting their team relegated to Division Three.

Games do not have to be occasions of great moment to live long in the memory. Most of the Cup finals I have seen have been forgettable, most European Cup finals doubly so. Still, I can sometimes remember names and dates. I can recite Cup final winners back to 1946, but even then I never know who won the Championship in any given year. Yet I can still remember, without trying, the exact date in December 1984 I saw Portsmouth play Oxford. The game sticks in the mind not because, played in torrential rain, it was of any great quality, but because Santa Claus ran on the pitch and Portsmouth scored the winner in the time added on for Santa's pitch invasion.

These are the things which constitute a life in football, not just *Match Of The Day*, the World Cup or *Abide With Me*. An afternoon at Gresty Road, when the away fans, afraid to miss a vital end-of-season match, were almost all inside by one o'clock, leaving them staring at three empty stands. The hour I spent standing in the rain on the Leazes End during a game at Newcastle which was abandoned at half-time. The day in which Oxford travelled to Tranmere and avoided relegation. The afternoon that Oxford lost to Marlow in the Cup.

I have been to Cup finals but I have fonder memories of a couple of cycling trips to Wycombe for away games, or an evening wandering drunk through Covent Garden after knocking Chelsea out of the Cup. A pub in Derby. Pubs in Brighton, in Swindon, in Wolverhampton. There are many grounds worth going to regardless of the standard of the game you watch, simply because of the standard of the pub you go to on the way. But you wouldn't, couldn't appreciate that watching at home on television.

Football is many different things. A Liverpool fan can appreciate Hartlepool just as a Hartlepool fan can appreciate Liverpool. It is not in the interest of football fans to play one level of football off against another, to decide that one is relevant and another doesn't matter. You wouldn't go to one and despise it for not being the other. You wouldn't want the one to destroy the other. But, however different they may be, you wouldn't want the links between the two to be broken. They are part of the same thing. While they are different, they are both the same.

In the Scottish League, clubs that hope to win European trophies are expected to compete with clubs for whom five-figure crowds are rare. That is the whole point. That is the beauty of this game, this international game, this game that revels in diversity. Would the FA Cup be a better competition if it were restricted to the Premiership, or only to the League? It might be more profitable to dispense with the tiresome business of wading through Preliminary Rounds, of letting clubs take part who have absolutely no chance of ever winning. It might be economically irrational to make Rangers play teams whose home support is rather less than Rangers' away following. Perhaps it is. So much the better if it is.

The point is that when we think about the game, and when we talk and write about it, what we discuss is far more interesting, far more diverse and pleasurable, than the narrow view of football in which the Premiership is interested. It has no place for the pleasures that are particular to small clubs playing for crowds of moderate size in pleasant towns. No place for the struggler, no place for the bad player and no place either for the relegated and despondent. No place for anything but the triumphant, the famous and the expensive. If these things go unheard of, if their important role in football goes unsaid, they will not survive. The Premiership doesn't want them. The television doesn't really want them either. Every current trend in football is against them. They are at genuine and serious risk.

There is much more to football than you can add up in pounds and pence, and if the Premiership, and television, have it all their own way, these things, which do not bring them revenue, will shrivel or will die. It is no good to say that the pubs round Griffin Park would still be there if Brentford closed, no good to say that Shrewsbury would be just as entertaining if they were playing part-time football in a future where professional football was limited to a few highly expensive franchises in our main cities. It would not be true. What was left *would* be a second-best where, at the moment, it is not.

This is something which is beginning to filter through to those parts of the press which have not abandoned everything to chase after the Premiership. It is hard to put your finger upon anything definite other than a certain enthusiasm for the Cup runs of 1997, for Stockport, Chesterfield, Falkirk and Kilmarnock. A growing, if still small, awareness of what was happening at Brighton, and a sympathy for the supporters there. A realisation that whereas most 'big' games are nothing of the sort, are just pumped up with too much hype and too much cliché, a game between Hereford and Brighton, in which the losers would drop out of the League, was something truly big, something historic, something moving. What matters it to Manchester United if one year they fail to win the Premiership? They'll be back to try again next year, and most likely will win it once again. It means nothing. Coming bottom meant something to Hereford. Promotion to the Premiership meant something to Barnsley.

Most of the glossy magazines may now go to Port Vale or Plymouth, but they would happily ditch either for an interview with David Beckham's girlfriends. Probably just as well. It is easy to see how football outside the Premiership could turn into a fad in just the way the Premiership did, a different sort of fad, a vehicle for another set of articles involving men examining their own inadequacies, a way for irritating students to show off, by coming to lower division grounds and laughing about how sad they think they are.

Even most of the less cynical, less trendy press still fail to understand. For my taste, too much of the enthusiasm for the smaller clubs is based on amazement, astonishment that clubs like Falkirk can beat clubs like Celtic. The effect is to magnify the gap rather than put it in perspective, to forget that clubs like Chesterfield still have professional players, players who should *expect* to win their games, to compete with their betters, to reach, to threaten to reach, semi-finals of serious competitions.

Still, it is better than nothing. It makes a difference. It matters how the media react to football, to changes that are happening, changes that are impending, in the game. They have a great deal of power to affect how people think about the game. They cannot determine how they think. They cannot *make* people understand what's happening to football, or make them understand that there is irreplaceable life outside the Premiership and that that life is under threat. But they can give them a chance of understanding it. They give them a chance of understanding what they stand to lose. They give them the chance of understanding how desperate the situation is, how late the hour.

If they do that, they give football a chance as well. It needs it. It needs people to speak up in its favour. We have no other way to influence the most powerful voices in the Premiership. We cannot appeal to their better nature. They have none. We cannot appeal to their wallets. Those wallets are doing very well the way things are right now.

Much of the life in football is being crushed out of it under the steamroller of commercialisation. We have to speak up for the diversity of football against the model that the City would prefer. We need to make our voices heard, heard against the prevailing wind, and heard, however difficult it seems, above the blare of television and the clang of the cash registers.

13. THE GLORY AND THE GREED

If you were to make a list of everything that bedevils football and put them in a pile, at the top of that pile would sit Manchester United. All the greed, all the arrogance, all the desperation to rip football away from its roots, are summed up in Manchester United. They have been the best team in the country over the last decade but they are also far ahead of everybody else in marketing and trivialising football, in shaping football for the benefit of the stock market, in squeezing every last penny of their pocket money from the nation's children.

To their supporters, like all supporters of all football clubs everywhere, what matters most is how the team get on. But what matters most to Old Trafford is how much money they can make. This is a club which makes more money from merchandising than it does from paying supporters, even though it already makes more money through the turnstiles than any other club. What sustains Manchester United is less its loyal support than its appeal to the child under peer-group pressure, to the glory-hunter, to the casual viewer gawping from their armchair. Their Premiership triumphs are only a means to an end, the end of greater souvenir sales and a rising share price. So if football supporters judge them more for their greed and exploitation than for their football, Manchester United can hardly complain. That is the way they also judge themselves.

There have been more successful clubs than Manchester United. There have been many better ones. But no football club before them has made money like Manchester United have made. They have made profits and lost friends in equal and unprecedented quantities. There has

101

never been anything like it in England before. No club has ever been disliked like Manchester United are disliked.

You don't even have to ask. You can start a conversation with another supporter, on the assumption that they like to see them beaten, and unless they actually support Manchester United, your assumption will, much more often than not, be right. There are few cheers on football grounds when the half-times are read out and they are winning, but if they are behind both sets of supporters are united in celebration of Manchester United's discomfort. Few people will even support them as the English representatives in Europe and, as a rule, the more dedicated and deeply involved the supporter, the more certain they are to be against them.

But the children love them. They have to. There is nothing like the pressure of your classmates, nothing like the allure of something bright, successful and on sale in the shops, to make up the minds of children for them. When I was a child replica shirts were unknown, but we did have wallcharts which depicted famous clubs and their traditional colours. Now the playground is full of little Giggses, Butts and Beckhams, but there are almost as many different colours to their shirts as there are children wearing them. Manchester United's colours do not remain traditional for more than six months at a time.

'You can only rip a person off once,' said Edward Freedman, their former director of marketing, contradicting the evidence of our eyes. New kits come out in January, just in time to render worthless the Christmas presents that these children's parents work hard to afford.

It has been alleged that much of their merchandise, manufactured in India, is made for next to nothing by young children. If this were true it would scarcely be the first time that Manchester United had exploited children. Manchester United argue that the sale of many different shirts only goes to show that they are meeting a demand. I could go to the same playground and shift a serious quantity of addictive drugs and then defend myself using the same justification. I doubt the public would accept my denial of responsibility. True, nobody is forced to buy their shirts (although the pleading of a child comes pretty close to *forced* in many people's minds) but by the same token, Manchester United are not forced to sell them, or to change them all the time. They know exactly what they're doing and what the consequences are, which is more than can be said for some of their customers.

They like to exploit their own supporters. Your chances of getting into Old Trafford without a season ticket are extremely slim. There are 40,000 season ticket holders, and only 10,000 seats reserved for members, of which there are 100,000. Neither seat tickets nor season tickets are among the cheapest in the Premiership, but Old Trafford may be the only ground in the country where it is actually expensive *not* to go. To become a member, to give yourself that ten per cent chance of buying a ticket, will cost you a tenner. Old Trafford bank a million pounds a season before they've even sold a ticket.

Manchester United have the largest Independent Supporters' Association in existence, and however many trophies their team win there is much for them to complain about. A club which has been known to throw supporters out for standing up is a club which thinks it can even tell its supporters how to support their team. If it doesn't like them, it can select its own supporters. It can replace them. It doesn't even have to replace them with people. In the Champions' League, they have taken to leaving seats unoccupied at the front of the stand so that the advertising hoardings appear more prominent on television.

They can price as many people out of Old Trafford as they want because there is a never-ending queue of people waiting to take their places. Freedman, asked if he was concerned that price rises were making it impossible for some supporters to watch the team, replied that he didn't see the problem because they could always watch the reserves for free. This is a club that treats supporters with contempt.

They treat the rest of football with contempt. They expect the rules to be changed for their convenience and on those rare occasions that they are not, they complain like spoiled children. In the run-in to their fourth Premiership title, Manchester United found themselves having to play more games than they might have liked, and demanded (*requested* would be too moderate a word) that the season be extended to accommodate them. When their demands were resisted they threw a fit. Ferguson attacked Roy Evans and Arsene Wenger for their temerity in suggesting that the rules were there and were the same for everyone.

It was just one episode of many, albeit a particularly ill-tempered and spectacular one. And an instructive one, demonstrating that no matter how much wealth or success a club accumulates, they will never stop believing that they are being hard done by. Indeed, the greater the wealth and the success, the more paranoid and arrogant that clubs become. They become so used to success that they regard it as their right. While Ferguson was throwing his tantrums, several other clubs, like Stockport and Stevenage, with far smaller squads than Ferguson had at his disposal, were actually playing more games in the season than Manchester United. Stockport County played 67 games that season. They got on with it, uncomplaining, in the professional manner.

Manchester United have too much arrogance and too much money at stake to show good manners or humility. This is a club which blamed a loss at Southampton on the confusion caused by the colour of the shirts they were wearing. A club whose manager complained that it was unfair that he had to play Liverpool the Saturday before a midweek European game. Nothing is more indicative of their arrogance than their contempt for the League Cup, in which they refuse to put out anything more than a token reserve side. If they ever wonder why they are resented by supporters, while the great Liverpool sides were mostly admired, they might remember that in 1984, when Liverpool won the Championship and the European Cup, they won the League Cup into the bargain. They played to win, like professionals, rather than hoping to get knocked out as soon as possible. Manchester United prefer to sulk and to complain that their burdens are too onerous.

That inability to win with grace is what has marked the Manchester United of the Nineties. It has contributed in no small way to their unpopularity. It ensures that their nastier aspects are remembered as much, and more, as the quality of their football. The viciousness with which Roy Keane deals with his opponents may not show up on a retrospective video, but if great Leeds or Arsenal sides are to be criticised for their cynicism then so should Manchester United. Eric Cantona's contribution on the field will not wipe from the memory his vanity and pretentiousness, nor the tendency he showed to stamp his studs on the chests of prone opponents.

It is not hard to think of reasons to dislike Manchester United. That dislike is often ascribed to jealousy. Good teams are not always popular. Arsenal were widely disliked during the Thirties, when they won three consecutive championships, for playing defensive football. But if it were jealousy, then all successful clubs would be disliked to the same extent. Liverpool, more successful than Manchester United have yet been, were not disliked very much at all. Supporters may have been bored by their string of championships and European Cups. They liked to see the Anfield machine get beaten. But there was none of the contempt, the automatic loathing which Manchester United attract.

Nor have all successful Manchester United sides attracted that loathing. The post-war side did not. The Busby Babes did not. Indeed there has been no more popular side in all the history of English football than the third Manchester United team Matt Busby built, the one which won the European Cup in 1968. Although much of their support today is owed to their domination of the Premiership, it also includes a large number of people who became attracted to them (or their parents did, and they continue the tradition) because of the great team of Charlton, Best and Law. These are the people who kept watching them during the 20 years in which they didn't win the title, let alone possess it as of right, and the people who kept on watching them even when they were relegated.

People like these are not glory-hunters. Nor are people who have followed them in Europe for the pleasure of having riot police crack their heads in Lisbon and in Istanbul. But there are a few who are. People from Surrey or Hertfordshire who call themselves supporters, watch an occasional game, or follow them on television, and then think that it reflects glory on them when they win again. If we were jealous, we would do exactly what they do, buy ourselves a satellite dish and a replica shirt and then congratulate ourselves on having chosen to 'support' the best. (You'd think we didn't realise that the clubs we follow are not likely to be as good as Manchester United are. Damn, here's me having picked Oxford to follow and all the time I never thought Manchester United would turn out the better team.)

Glory-hunters get up our noses, lording it over people who follow their local teams. It is a shallow, sad way to watch if all you understand about the game, if all you want from it, is a constant stream of victories and trophies. Glory-hunters irritate the rest of us and as there are more at Manchester United than at any other club, it follows that we dislike Manchester United all the more for it.

The army of glory-hunters contribute to the mood against Manchester United but they can't entirely explain it. Its very uniqueness, its depth and its extent, means it can't be down to jealousy. What explains it is that the accusations made against them are basically true. They are greedy. They are exploitative. They are as ungracious as they are arrogant. They are all these things and more, and they possess these negative qualities in greater depth than any club before them.

The times are at fault as much as the club. The times have helped to make the club the bloated monster that it is. The times have taken clubs away from their cities and made them into placeless, rootless constructs, whose geographical location is no longer of any real relevance to who they are. Manchester United are less and less anything to do with the city of Manchester, with an upbringing in that city, or with the experience of life there. Manchester United are their sales and their trophies. That is all they are. There is a vacuum where their sense of identity should be. That is both their success and the emptiness inside it. That emptiness is not unique to Manchester United.

Already, ten years ago, 50 per cent of Liverpool's home support came from more than 30 miles away from Anfield. The figure is unlikely to be lower now. Chelsea are notoriously detached from the area of West London where they play. House prices in the immediate area are probably too expensive even for those who can afford a season ticket in the East Stand. Arsenal and Tottenham, supposedly the fiercest of local rivals, are in reality practically identical in terms of the catchment area of their support. This or that area may lean to Highbury or White Hart Lane, but either club is as much to do with St Albans, or Stevenage, as it is to do with Haringey or Finsbury Park.

Liverpool will never embody their city again like they did when Shankly built the club. Newcastle, or even Wolverhampton, might aspire to that mantle. But Newcastle exclude too many supporters for anyone to feel that they really represent the working people of Newcastle any more. And Wolves, presumably, would have to be similarly transformed if they wanted to maximise their revenue to compete with the élite.

Identity and local pride are now an obstacle to be overcome, a skin which clubs prefer to shed. When Chelsea won the FA Cup, there was a bus ride, a reception, in the area of Stamford Bridge, but there was something hollow about it, a feeling that the crowds as much as the players had been brought in for the occasion, that they lived, like most Chelsea fans do, nowhere near Chelsea. If Middlesbrough had won it would have been different. But Middlesbrough are about Middlesbrough and that, something which would have sustained them in the past, will forever prevent them gaining a long-term place among the élite.

The biggest football clubs now stand alone from their supporters, who are replaceable, from their localities, which are irrelevant, and from the rest of football, which is merely an irritation. It is a grotesque and impersonal circus, as lacking in substance as it is bountiful in income. It consists only of itself. It exists only for itself. It is a world of its own. Manchester United are the leaders of this trend, its symbol. It is not jealousy which has turned supporters against Manchester United. It is bitterness and it is sadness.

It is sadness at what football has become. Football supporters love the game of football. Among the many things we love about it is that we love to see it played as well as football can be played. With skill, with courage, with exuberance, with wit, with application and professionalism. We prefer to love our football than to hate it. We would prefer to admire Manchester United than to resent them.

Because they have been, without question, an admirable team, whatever their less appealing qualities, whatever their deficiencies, whatever their lack of grace in victory and in chasing victory. There is a growing difference, at Old Trafford and everywhere else, between the *team* and the *club*. The team, for all their faults, may be wonderful, but we cannot help thinking of the club, and that sours it, it spoils it for everybody.

The money spoils it. It gets in the way of everything. Nobody knows how good Alex Ferguson is. We cannot tell. However good he is, the fact that he can make mistakes worth millions and then spend further millions to put them right will always influence our judgement. We cannot judge him properly against his contemporaries, or against his fellow managers from the past. Plainly he owes his success to more than spending money. But plainly money has made a major contribution. Few of the players he has really wanted have not signed for him. Of English players, only Alan Shearer really comes to mind. Ferguson's achievement has been considerable. But we have lost it among the blizzard of money which Old Trafford represents.

We have lost Manchester United among all the magazines and cards and shirts and videos and clocks, and other souvenirs. We do not know what they are any more. A football team? A leisurewear company? A leading player in the entertainment industry? Some years ago, when Liverpool were the fashion among children, a friend of mine commented that if you only wanted to support success, you might as well support the Hanson Trust instead. And now our élite clubs resemble blue-chip companies, their names trademarks, their goals financial, their business business.

We have lost Manchester United and the other élite clubs who resemble them. We have lost these clubs and they have lost interest in us. We are not part of them, they are not part of us. They are interested only in themselves. They pursue that self-interest aggressively. That is the difference. The Liverpool myth wore off when they started selling shirts around the country, when not only were they ceasing to be about Liverpool but they were ensuring that other clubs felt strangers in their own backyards. As much as anything, it is the feeling of being permanently embattled, of trying to fight a rising tide of all things Manchester United, which makes it impossible to like them now.

Manchester United won their popularity, they earned their popularity because of what they did decades ago in Europe. Because of the vision of Matt Busby, because of the skill and will with which that vision was successfully pursued, because that vision was conceived of in terms of sporting achievement, not in terms of television revenue and an upward movement on the Stock Exchange. When Manchester United play in

Europe now, English supporters, in large numbers, support the other side. That is the distance that football has come.

Manchester United are presented as a shining example of what football can achieve, as the leaders of the English game, a symbol of everything to which other clubs should aspire. They are not. They are a symbol of what has gone wrong with football, an object lesson in the victory of money over football and in the unpopularity with football supporters that results. As such, they merely are a symbol of how football has gone sour.

14. THE DISSATISFIED CUSTOMER

The image that suits Manchester United best is not the team, nor Old Trafford, nor even the century of history behind the club. It is the Superstore outside Old Trafford and its constant stream of customers. It is so easy to give your money to Manchester United. There are little versions of their Superstore in towns across the country. Manchester United are as visible as McDonalds or Coca-Cola, and, within their own commercial sector, just as powerful. In their own way they are as much a triumph of free-market capitalism as the end of Eastern Europe or the Blairing of the Labour Party. They think of nothing else but how to get more customers through the doors more often. Why doesn't Old Trafford sell *all* its seats to season ticket holders? The demand is certainly there. Martin Edwards has the explanation: 'The "floaters" are the ones who go to the shop and buy the souvenirs.' Clever. Manchester United refuse consumer demand in one area, the better to increase it somewhere else. Whatever rings up the most net sales is what is best for Old Trafford. That is how they measure their success.

A success is a sale. That is the rule by which the market works, the only rule by which it works. Those who sell the most are by that rule the best. Those who don't have failed because they got it wrong. The customer is king and the market has to give us what we want at a price that we can pay. In that way it ensures that we get what we want and society is satisfied.

But society is not satisfied. It teems with dissatisfaction. Those needs that are met are artificial, while our real needs go unrecognised and unmet by the provision that the market makes. You cannot really

109

measure human needs and emotions in the currency of cash transactions. You cannot put people at ease by forcing them to compete with one another. This is true of the provision of food for all, and medicine, and shelter. Next to these things, football is of minuscule importance. But the market fails in football as it does elsewhere.

It fails because the premises on which it is based are myths. The myth is that those who succeed do so because they emerge successful from free competition. In football this is nonsense. The competition is totally unequal. The myth is that ordinary people exercise their power as consumers, condemning those they do not want by going elsewhere with their money. The football supporter does not behave like that. The myth is that as we are the customers, we can demand a high standard of service. But football supporters are still treated abysmally. The myth is that the drive to compete increases the level of production. Yet the likelihood is that we are likely to have less football in the future, not more.

We are not customers. We do not want to be. We do not behave like customers are supposed to behave. Those who succeed by running football clubs do not succeed by winning the battle for our custom, but by picking a sure thing and spending money on it. The complacency of those who run them is the complacency of those who cannot lose, not of those who have fought hard to get where they are. The more market-orientated football has become, the *less* stringent the competition has become. These clubs are no more troubled by competition than are Proctor and Gamble. To make a success of Tottenham is rather easier than it was to make a success of Amstrad.

At the top, real failure is becoming almost unknown. If the influence of the market were to make football more competitive, you would expect movement in and out of the top positions in the game to be faster and more frequent. The opposite has proved to be the case. The chairmen of the richest clubs congratulate themselves on their success. They would have more justification in congratulating themselves on their failure. It would be harder to achieve.

In the world of football, as business sees it, if clubs like Exeter or Lincoln struggle to survive while Arsenal and Chelsea thrive, it is because Exeter and Lincoln didn't come up with the goods. They do not deserve to survive because they haven't proved themselves in the marketplace. That is not just a callous attitude, it is a meretricious one. If John Hall thinks he knows so much about how to make a football club successful, I'd like to see him repeat the trick at Hartlepool. All he had to do at Newcastle was to spend a lot of money and understand a little about marketing. Would that be enough to make a success of Hartlepool? Of Mansfield? Of Exeter?

How on earth are Exeter supposed to compete with Arsenal? You may as well expect a corner shop to compete with Tesco. If anything, it would be easier for the corner shop. Exeter have no chance of competing. It is a simple matter of demographics. There may be in excess of ten million people living within an hour and a half's travelling time of Highbury. Within the same distance of St James's Park there must be fewer than a million. You could hardly have a playing field less level than that.

Even if we were talking about Barnet, whose ground, to those ten million, is almost as accessible as Arsenal's, how are they to suddenly acquire the capital to make a real competition possible? What would they need? Two or three hundred million pounds for start-up costs? Then another 20 million or so a year, and a willingness to keep that spending up for a couple of decades, until they had created as many traditional Barnet supporters as there are Arsenal fans. You might as well ask them to play their home games on the moon.

Competition is a nonsense because clubs don't genuinely compete among themselves for supporters. They might occasionally compete for customers for their souvenirs. If Liverpool displace Manchester United from their dominant position, then perhaps the nation's children will go back to wearing shirts that advertise Carlsberg rather than Sharp. The very few clubs that can compete for this sort of custom are clubs who are already safe from the rigours of competition. Occasionally the élite clubs may lose an infinitesimal number of supporters to whatever hometown clubs are doing better than they used to be. When Bradford do well, they attract a number of supporters who might otherwise have been tempted in the direction of Elland Road. But it is never more than temporary. In the long run Leeds will always be a bigger club than Bradford and those people who prefer to travel to watch big-city clubs will always do so.

Supporters are not real customers. Customers make choices, supporters do not. The very existence of a competitive market assumes, and requires, real and free choices to be made by customers. If Sainsbury aren't up to the mark, we go to Tesco. If a restaurant displeases us, we go somewhere else next time. If football supporters do not behave the same way, do not exercise choice, the consumer model of football falls apart.

We make a small number of choices. We are less likely to go to away games when the team is losing, less likely to renew our season tickets when the team is relegated. But we are not likely to shop elsewhere. We do *not* go elsewhere when we are dissatisfied. We may miss home games now and then, but most of the time, regardless of results, we will not. When we do, it may be more down to shortage of money, which gives us no choice at all, than to our choosing to spend our money somewhere else. We may stay away out of disgust but most of us would rather stay home than watch another team, let alone support them.

I would watch Oxford even if they were relegated to the Conference, rather than go to London, just an hour away, to watch Premiership football. In fact, were I to move to London I imagine I would come to Oxford rather than watch some other club in London, no matter how much better they were than Oxford. How can we be customers? We do not exercise choice. We actively refuse it.

Who wants to be a customer anyway? Football supporters complain, rightly, that we pay good money and deserve better in return. But we should be wary of seeing ourselves as dissatisfied consumers, of seeing football as a financial transaction between a seller and a buyer. Our relationship with football is a closer one than can be added up in pounds and pence. Moreover, if we expect to be put first *as customers*, then we can't complain if other people spend more than us and are then put ahead of us. If other people will happily pay more for their tickets than we can, we can't complain about a rip-off. And there are, additionally the many other people who buy football. The City buys football. The TV companies buy football. The sponsors and the advertisers buy football. They are all far more powerful customers than we are. If the customer is always right, to which customer is football going to refer?

Value for money depends on how much money you are spending. You get what you pay for and only that. A higher ticket price should have paid for an improvement in facilities but evidently prices are still not high enough. You pay the earth to watch a team of millionaires but still get food that would be better left uneaten. It may come from a kiosk rather than a wooden hut and they'll let you have it in a polystyrene box. But it is still disgusting.

I wonder what the food is like in the executive boxes. I wonder how long the people in them have to queue for the toilet. Not long ago I went to Highfield Road to watch Coventry. On the stroke of the half-time whistle, the queue for the gents was, already, far longer than a cricket pitch. You exercised a choice all right, to either miss the toilets or miss some of the match. Highfield Road is not unusual. Toilets cost money and organising access to them requires some thought. Football begrudges the first and has little to spare of the second. We don't usually even think about it. We are used to it, just like we were used to the pissoir round the back of the Linthorpe Road at Ayresome Park, like we were used to the urinals at Roots Hall which were open to inspection by the public. (And, as far as I know, they still are.)

Football clubs are always going to skimp on toilets, food, turnstiles, ticket information, anything that costs them money but might add to our comfort. There are sports stadiums in America where people are treated like people deserve to be. But they are mostly the province of the affluent middle-class who can afford a ticket price that might make even Chelsea blush. That is the customer's catch-22. We can only have these things if they are so expensive that we can't afford them. We should talk the language of entitlement, not of the customer. We should demand that everybody is entitled to the best facilities available, no matter how much money, or how little, they have got.

Our money doesn't buy the concern of football clubs. The more they make from us, the more they can ignore us. They don't spend much money making it easier for us. Phoning up the richer clubs for a ticket is like phoning up one of those faceless companies with automatic switchboards and a muzak tape to listen to while you wait. You wait for ages, while they tempt you with an 0891 number offering ticket information at premium prices. Élite clubs that make millions still begrudge the few thousand a year it costs to hire ticket office staff. Why should they care how long you wait? If you don't want to, others will.

Still less does anyone care about the travelling supporter. The home club doesn't and nobody else will when nobody else is making any money out of us. Games are rearranged with no thought for the arrangements made by travelling supporters. Games are abandoned or postponed at the last possible minute. Otherwise programmes would have to be pulped, tickets reprinted, even, horror of horrors, refunds made. One Oxford game, at Watford, was called off one minute before kick-off. Abandonments are made, or not made, specifically without reference to the point of view of the paying supporter. If the referee can see, no matter how little the supporters can see through the fog, then the game goes on. But if the referee decides to abandon it, we can usually whistle for a refund.

You can't imagine that if a cinema failed to show a film, if the projector broke down halfway through, it could refuse an instant refund to the punters. But football supporters rarely qualify for refunds or compensation. The most outrageous recent example was the occasion when Scotland's game in Estonia was called off, after the kick-off time was changed at the last moment and the home side failed to turn up. The home supporters were ill-served by the decision to move the kick-off, leaving them holding tickets for a game supposed to take place while

113

they were at work. But the away supporters had paid hundreds of pounds to follow their team to Tallinn. Nobody thought of compensating them for their wasted journey, their considerable expense. If UEFA had properly assessed the floodlights, or if it had not panicked and moved the kick-off time, there would have been no wasted journeys and no useless tickets. But however much money UEFA makes, it didn't have enough to compensate fans for losses caused by its incompetence.

Football does not value its supporters. It mostly resents them, especially when they are ungrateful enough to complain. Birmingham City were taken to court for adding an illegal surcharge to the price of tickets for away games. When they lost the case, they reacted by taking away the season ticket of the fan who had complained. They had the stewards escort him from the ground. Never mind that he was right, never mind his many years putting money into the club. In throwing him out they were only acting out the fantasy of other clubs who would love to do the same to all their whingeing fans.

They resent us, even though they are sitting pretty. We have all the disadvantages of being a customer and none of the advantages. By contrast, they have it both ways. When they succeed, they can replace us with a better off, less recalcitrant customer. But when they fail, and the fly-by-nights fly elsewhere, they have us to fall back on, always ready to complain, but always willing to pay them for the privilege. We are a licence to print money. If Manchester United were to briefly slip from the élite, Old Trafford would still be packed, but with a different sort of fan than those whose spending potential they aim to tap today. The club would look on them as second best, but they would come nevertheless. We are football's fallback position, its lifetime guarantee, and they know it. They have us where they want us. They, not the customers, are king.

The change in the conditions of supporters in the last few years is that we find ourselves paying more for football than we used to. That is the final disproof of the market model. Prices are supposed to fall. Competition between supermarkets brings down the price of food. Competition between bus companies brings down the price of public transport. Competition between suppliers brings down the price of gas. That is the theory. But letting market forces rip in football has only succeeded in inflating prices. We have the right to spend our money where we see fit. We have the choice to spend our money as we choose. But in reality we have little choice and very few rights.

The owners of the Superstores, not the supporters, call the tune. Football is set up the way they want it, not the way we'd like it. Does anybody feel that, as customers, we're in control? Does anybody feel that, as they make more money out of us, they are much more solicitous for our welfare? Power is not in our hands but in the hands of the owners, and they know it. They are going to make us pay for it.

15. A CONSTRUCTIVE DEBATE

Such are the threats hovering over football, such the impositions it lays on its supporters that even where there have been improvements these do not seem to count for very much. A few players of world class don't make a lot of difference when most of us don't get to see them. Wider television coverage is not much help if it becomes more expensive to actually watch it. And the many ground improvements, the shiny new stadia, new stands, new seats, are not always as wonderful as their brightness and their cleanliness suggests. We have had to pay a lot of money to see these stands erected and these seats installed, and in a mundane sort of way that tends to take the edge off any pleasure we might otherwise feel. We get nothing for nothing. Anyone who goes to a new ground, or to a new stand in an old ground, knows what the likely implications are for ticket prices.

Still football grounds, by and large, are in a better state now than they were ten years ago. The changes shouldn't be exaggerated. People who only watch the Premiership may only see the new, may not realise how much of the old is with us still. Many grounds have barely altered from the state they were in before the commercial boom, and before the Taylor Report. Stands deemed unsafe are no longer used, even if they are still left standing. But it is not yet a different world. More grounds than not still have terraces. They are not some relic, some bizarre but rare survival from a distant past. At a rough guess, perhaps a quarter of supporters, in the four divisions, still stand up to watch. If others had the choice, it might be many more.

Not all that much has changed. Nor are the changes as beneficial as they ought to be. The removal of the terraces remains a thorny issue, an unsatisfactory solution. The bright appearance of new stands often belies cramped conditions, poor sightlines and insufficient protection from the weather. The new constructions are too often dull, designed without imagination, located without ambition. There is much about contemporary football which is nothing more than hype and sham. The rebuilding of stadia is not like that. It represents a genuine improvement. But what is good about it is not necessarily what is supposed to be good about it, and what is supposed to be better is often no improvement at all.

Some of the rebuilt grounds are certainly so much better than the old grounds as to be literally unrecognisable. Whatever problems remain at Highfield Road, it has still changed so much that visiting for the first time since 1988, I was unable to work out which end, on the previous occasion, I had been standing on. At Stamford Bridge, the old North Terrace, one of the most notorious eyesores in the game, is gone. It used to be a huge, uncovered, crumbling terraced curve on which, no matter how small the travelling support, the Metropolitan Police would invite you to come down and watch from right at the front. You stood behind a fence where you could hardly see the game but they could easily see you. Now the North Terrace is the new North Stand. You would not believe you were in the same place. And if £20 to sit in it is still extortionate, it's almost worth it just to know we'll never see that North Terrace again.

There have been some spectacular improvements. Molineux has been turned into the sort of ground that their supporters deserve, in place of the derelict bomb site they put up with for years. For all the financial problems that the New Den has caused Millwall, at least nobody has to watch the game while standing directly behind a floodlight pylon, like they did at Cold Blow Lane. The Intel Stand at Swindon lacks the charm of the old Shrivenham Road but games no longer have to be postponed because a high wind might blow down the stand. Home fans who can afford to go to Newcastle are no longer insulted by there being no roof on the Gallowgate.

Football grounds are better to look at than they were. Yet too often, if we ask more of them than cleanliness and newness, they do not have much more to offer. They are not all that much to look at. Some of the new stands may be impressive, in a forceful sort of way, but none are particularly imaginative. They do not have the character, still less the idiosyncrasy, of the intruding buildings at Craven Cottage and at Goodison, the criss-cross frontages that Archibald Leitch created at

Ibrox, Goodison and several other grounds, the 16-foot slope which gave Wycombe's old Loakes Park what charm it possessed, or even the little jumble of stands on the Cuckoo Lane at the Manor Ground.

Bescot Stadium, consisting of four practically identical stands, is rendered even duller by comparison with the striking RAC building a short distance up the road. Worse than dullness is the lack of originality on offer. Some of the smaller new grounds look like easy-to-assemble versions of each other. The Deva Stadium and Adams Park could be swapped over without making much difference.

How football grounds look, and where they are, are not important issues compared to whether they are safe. But if we were buying a house, we wouldn't ignore its appearance or its surroundings, provided we were persuaded that it wasn't going to fall down. It is disappointing that this revolution in our conditions has to be so mediocre in imagination. Outside the ring road is no place for a football ground. A stadium ripped away from the city it is supposed to serve, away from the people and the pubs, is a stadium dull to visit, a stadium divorced from the city life of which it ought to be a part. Adams Park is right down the end of an industrial estate, as far away as possible from stations, pubs, amenities and people. Sixfields, right on the edge of Northampton, ringed by roundabouts and wasteland, shares space with Burger King, a multiplex cinema and a hideous theme pub. But at least it doesn't smell. Oxford chose a site on which to build a new ground which is adjacent to, and downwind of, the city's sewage works.

The rebuilding of grounds has been a wasted opportunity, failing to ask, let alone answer, a lot of questions which it had the opportunity to ask, questions about football's relationship to the cities in which it makes its home, questions about what football grounds are capable of becoming, not just what particular evils need to be avoided.

Most of all, it has failed to ask the question of what supporters really want. You cannot discuss the rebuilding of stadia without confronting the question of the all-seater requirement and whether it was really necessary. And you cannot discuss that question without accepting that nobody ever really asked supporters whether they thought the terraces should be got rid of. The terraces were outlawed in the Premiership and, theoretically, in Division One, against the will of many of the fans who wanted them to stay.

This is supposed to have been left behind us in the past, something settled and done with, something on which everybody is agreed. Yet it is not. The terraces are not forgotten even by those who have been forced to sit for several years. The Football Supporters' Association, driven by its members' discontent, has called for a partial return to terracing. Tom Pendry MP, Shadow Minister for Sport prior to Labour taking power, and for ten years football supporters' best friend in the Commons, made the same suggestion early in 1997.

For his pains he was frostily received. Anybody who dares ask whether the replacement of terraces was actually the right way forward, runs the risk of being cast as someone unconcerned about the safety of supporters, someone who has forgotten Hillsborough. Or of being someone unduly attached to the terrace culture of the Seventies, with all its attendant hooliganism and discomfort. These are not serious arguments, however often they are used. They are ways of deploying abuse in order to avoid debate.

No one is more concerned about the safety of football grounds than the supporters. They do not need to be lectured about dangers of which they were aware many years before the authorities took any notice. Those of us who are unconvinced about the Taylor Report do not disagree because we would prefer some lifestyle out of *Zigger Zagger*, because we hanker after a life of running, kicking and being kicked, because we are disinterested in the creation of safe conditions for supporters. The suggestion is both dishonest and offensive.

No less offensive is the caricature of terrace life which is often counterposed to the different atmosphere of the seats. I have lost count of the number of references I have read to the rivers of urine that apparently flowed endlessly on football terraces, as if it used to be compulsory when standing at a football match either to piss in someone else's pocket or have somebody else piss into yours. I have to say that I have been watching football for 15 years, standing on terraces for all that time, and never once in my recollection have I seen so much as a drop of urine on a football terrace.

It is possible that these things did happen in the past. They might have occurred not because of the non-existence of seats, but because of the non-existence of toilets (unless we are suggesting that the sort of people who prefer terraces to seats are the sort of people who prefer not to use toilets). So it is an argument about toilets, not an argument about terraces. Or they might have occurred because, when terraces were grossly overcrowded, those toilets were out of reach to many of the fans packed in too tightly. That is an argument about capacity, not an argument about terraces.

Anyway, it should be quite evident that to argue for terraces is not to argue for terraces unchanged in construction from the past. It is to argue for terraces with much reduced capacities and much increased provision of exits and crash barriers. These are measures which have, in fact, been implemented. It has to be accepted that supporters can make an honest case against compulsory seating. When that is accepted, then an honest discussion of how we can make grounds safer can be had. But it is a discussion which has never taken place.

The Taylor Report, famously and I think wrongly, recommended that every football ground should become all-seater. Taylor's was not a totally uninformed report. But it reaches its conclusion without considering any other possible judgement. It sums up in a solitary sentence. 'It is obvious that sitting for the duration of the match is more comfortable than standing. It is also safer.' (Taylor Report, paragraph 63) *It is obvious*. It does not require debate.

Having already come to his conclusion, Taylor does go on, in that same paragraph, to explain it. There would be less jostling and no swaying or moving. But he presents no arguments to the contrary, even in order to refute them. The objections to all-seaters which he examines are those of tradition, reduced capacity and cost (paragraphs 66-72), and do not, at any point, touch on any safety problems with all-seaters or on any quarrel with his doubts about the safety of terraces. It is a debate in which only one side is permitted to speak.

Even then, his argument, which he assumes to be a statement of the obvious, is no such thing. 'Sitting . . . is more comfortable than standing.' Is it really? If Taylor had argued that the *comfort* of the spectator were of no importance relative to their *safety*, he would have been on firmer, indeed unchallengeable ground. As it is, his assertion is nonsense. Seats are not more comfortable than terraces. Many people may prefer them, for the reasons that he gives or for other reasons of comfort, because, for instance, they provide relief from fatigue. But many others do not prefer them precisely because they are not comfortable. Seats are cramped, but legs freed to walk and move are not. If Taylor felt that seating was more comfortable, someone should have taken him to watch Luton Town from the Oak Road seats after it was converted from terracing. Only a particularly small and stoic child could sit in those seats without complaining of cramp. The Oak Road seats are not atypical. The case can be made that seats are safer. But the case that they are more comfortable is rather harder to accept.

Taylor made assumptions which he should not have made. Not because he didn't care about supporters. He was concerned about the question of what it would cost supporters financially if terraces were replaced. 'Spectators do not want to pay, and, it is argued, many could not pay the substantially higher price of a seat' (paragraph 69). He comments sympathetically that 'it should be possible to plan a price structure which suits the cheapest seats to the pockets of those presently paying to stand' (paragraph 72), which, to put it mildly, is precisely what has not happened. If clubs that have rebuilt at our expense say they have only been doing what the Taylor Report suggested, then they have only read those parts of the Report which suited them.

But we should not be too kind to Taylor. He may have wanted ticket prices to be kept down but he made no such suggestion among his 76 recommendations. In leaving the issue aside in this way he gave the clubs carte blanche to roll over their supporters. In practice clubs have been free to do precisely what he hoped they wouldn't. Perhaps he didn't see it coming. In his discussion of how ground improvements might be financed (paragraphs 99-130) he has no inkling that in fact, the pockets of supporters will be the major source of capital.

There is much about the subject of football stadia that Taylor did not understand. He fails to grasp that safety objections exist to all-seater stands as well as to the terraces. Seats may reduce the problems caused by crowd pressure but they produce their own problems. They make access and egress more difficult. This can be a matter of life and death. If the Bradford fire had happened in a terraced stand, the loss of life would have been far smaller. It takes seconds to run from one end of a terrace to another but minutes to climb over rows of seats. That proved too long for those who died at Valley Parade.

Certainly, if rubbish had not been dumped under the stand, or if it had not been constructed out of wood, the tragedy would have been avoided. But that is to say no more than if there had not been fences at Hillsborough, that tragedy would have been avoided too. Seats make it harder to get in and out, and Taylor never considers the problems that this poses. Sometimes people collapse at grounds. It is often cold at matches. People go to watch when they are ill. Old people make up a fair proportion of the crowd. I have seen fans collapse, both on terraces and among the seats. On terraces it is a great deal easier for the St John's Ambulance staff to get to them and get them out.

These questions are not trivial. Their implications for the safety of all-seater grounds can be minimalised by intelligent design and considerate planning, but they will always exist. But the same is true of terraces which have been made far safer than they were. The surges that occurred before have gone and it is hard to see where the momentum for a crush can come from now. It might happen within a tunnel, or a walkway, but these are as much features of all-seater grounds as of any other kind.

It would be stupid to be complacent. Not least because we know clubs drag their feet over safety procedures, fail to train stewards, let basic guidelines go ignored. But most of the complacency appears to be on the side of the new stands. Are their walkways, narrow, crowded, enclosed, claustrophobic, all as safe as they ought to be? Is there really no danger of trampling in the event of panic? Could they be efficiently evacuated if a fire started in the fast-food outlets? They do not make me as nervous as I used to be when being crushed by a surge but, in an emergency, I would be happier on any terrace now than on these walkways.

It is so important to be able to get out. That is why the fences had to go. Without them, the pens at Hillsborough could have simply emptied on to the pitch. Nothing worse than an interrupted game would have resulted. The Taylor Report does not say nearly enough about fences. What should have been a report about fences became a report about terraces. It makes eight recommendations with respect to fences, but it does not require that they be removed. It abolishes the terrace and moderates the problems caused by the fence, whereas it should have been the other way round.

Possibly Taylor was reluctant to overturn completely the law-and-order emphasis which, until the Report was published, constituted the entirety of social policy where football was concerned. This was the age of the ID card and the Luton experiment. (I saw several games at Kenilworth Road when away supporters were supposedly excluded. There were always a fair number there. Rather than Luton being the only League club to keep away fans out, they were the only one without segregation! This was a fact avoided in the press, both then and since.)

Taylor criticised the police, as judicial enquiries occasionally do, but he was never going to be inclined to identify the police as the problem, or indeed to take issue with the policing of supporters generally, without which discussion the rationale for fencing us in could not be properly debated. Given those limitations, there was practically no option but to identify the terrace as the problem. It is not a question of sincerity. Taylor honestly believed the terrace ought, for our safety, to be eradicated. But his report was limited in scope, in perception, and we need to be aware of that.

From Taylor the matter was passed to the Home Secretary and to Parliament, which followed the Home Secretary in accepting the Report in full. I do not blame them one bit. Hillsborough was fresh in their memories. Nobody wished to question recommendations which were aimed at preventing a repeat of that tragedy. But in consequence there was no debate about whether Taylor was right. There was plenty of discussion in fanzines and among supporters generally. But we were little consulted (there was some small FSA input into the Taylor Inquiry, but it did not at all sway Taylor's thinking) and where it mattered, the case against the terraces went by default.

It has been argued that without the Taylor Report, football clubs would have continued to ignore the dangers to which they were subjecting their supporters. There is no doubt that this is true. Much good has come of Taylor even though his analysis was flawed. But that does not mean that the Report should be treated as infallible. Supporters are quite capable of discussing safety requirements without taking it as gospel. There must be room for us to engage in independent thought.

If supporters' opinions were canvassed, there might be something done about the shoddiness with which some clubs have implemented the recommendations of the Report. Some clubs have been all law and no spirit, putting in seats without proper consideration of the comfort of supporters. From Luton Town to Wembley, at many different football grounds, they skimp at our expense. Among the worst examples is the Stratton Bank at Swindon.

'Standing on an exposed terrace on a wet day is uncomfortable, sitting in the rain is worse.' Paragraph 63 of the Report, a paragraph which Swindon seemed to have missed the last couple of times I was at the County Ground. Plastic seats with no back and with no roof to cover them. Bird droppings everywhere, making it unpleasant if not impossible to sit down. If you could, then in the cold and rain it would be a thoroughly nasty experience. As you can't, the situation is no better than before, except that some people get a better view by balancing on the seats. This is not more comfortable nor is it safer. But every one of Taylor's actual recommendations has been met.

The Taylor Report, whatever its inadequacies, was intended as a way to make us safer. But it has been implemented in a partial manner, meanly, thoughtlessly, and then used as a means to rip us off again. In that context why should we simply submit to the imposition of all-seaters? Why should we pay more for something that we did not ask for, something we do not want and which many well-informed supporters do not believe we need?

Of course as much seating as is required has to be provided. Many people prefer to pay for seats. It is a more convenient and comfortable way for families to attend. Family seating should be available at a price that working-class families might be able to afford. For those who want to sit and have the money to pay for expensive tickets, fine. Provide seating at whatever price they are prepared to pay. Many older people prefer to sit and they must be accommodated too.

But just because some people have a distaste for terraces and others have a distaste for the people who stood, and stand, on them, that is no excuse for wiping us from history as if we deserved no say in the matter. Let the supporters talk about it. Let us discuss it. It is, is it not, *our* safety that is at stake?

16. LESSONS UNLEARNED

Of everything from the Eighties that has not changed significantly, the policing of football stands out. It is still aggressive, still overbearing, still as hostile to supporters as it was before. If it has changed at all, it is only that it has become more technological, more concerned with cameras and helicopters, less reliant on the physical presence of large numbers of uniformed police. But what presence there is has not, visibly, improved its attitude towards supporters. The main difference is that the police are now allowed, legally, to do most of the things they used to do whether they were legal or not.

Inside football grounds we see less of the police than we used to. This is partly because cameras now carry out the role of surveillance, officers usually only being mobilised when crowd tension is evident or when snatch squads are deemed to be required. It is partly because the police are so expensive that many clubs prefer, on grounds of cost, to use stewards inside the ground. But it is also because there is a tacit recognition of the mutual distrust between supporters and the police, an understanding that fans prefer to be politely searched by someone in an orange coat than manhandled by someone in a uniform.

If anything, we are too used to the police's role in football, too accustomed to what they do, when we really ought to question how much they are needed. Some years ago I was aggressively searched outside the County Ground in Swindon (hat wrenched off head to search for weapons, coat pulled open without asking first). Later in the week, I found myself talking about it to a friend – a manager and a Conservative voter. He was shocked. Not by the nature of the search but by the fact that people were searched just because they were entering a football ground. I tried to persuade him that we took it for granted, that we accepted it, but he would have none of it. Perhaps, at that time, we were so used to believing that we were, as supporters, publicly despised that we didn't think it worth making a fuss about how we were treated. But now we have been accepted back into society, we should make that fuss a whole lot more.

Whenever the role of the police in football is discussed, it is customary to observe that they have a difficult job and that we would not want to do it. They do indeed have a difficult job. I would not want to do it. I do not fancy being cooped up for hours in a hot transit van with a dozen other officers, and I would rather watch the match than the crowd. But if the police have a difficult job, it is a job they often do very badly.

Certainly, some supporters who find themselves in conflict with the police are indeed hooligans. There are still a few about (and at some local derbies, and end-of-season matches, more than a few). But most supporters are not hooligans and never were, and police operations at football matches are not as good as they ought to be at distinguishing between the two.

The police are rarely well-informed about the grounds which they police. They know where and when they expect the supporters to arrive, where trouble may be expected, what routes home the away fans take. But ask where you find the correct entrance for your ticket, the sort of straightforward question that supporters ask, and they do not often know. This only matters, because it matters what the police are briefed about. It matters what role they think they are playing, whether they are serving and helping the public or merely keeping them in order.

In theory, the policing of a football match may be a tremendously sophisticated operation, involving all sorts of prior intelligence, taking into account all sorts of variables about the likely behaviour of different sections of the crowd. In practice, it is a crude and inflexible operation involving a very few simple preconceptions about football supporters.

Problems are assumed to mostly derive from the travelling supporters. Any fan who goes to both home and away matches knows how differently you are treated. Away supporters are more rigorously searched. They are ejected for behaviour that goes unnoticed in the home end, and they are still occasionally marched *en masse* from ground to station. Yet there are few reasons to expect away fans to be inherently more interested in causing trouble than the home fans. And if the police are acting to a fixed plan, and that plan is itself based on false premises, then the police will make a mess of it, however many cameras, vans and officers they have available.

Very often they make a total hash of it and then make it worse by panicking when they ought to stay calm. They react late and then lash out at random. The worst example I have personally witnessed in the last few years involved a game at Huddersfield not long after the new stadium had been opened. It was not yet completely finished, so both sets of fans were seated in the same stand, sharing the same facilities and exits. When they all left the ground at the same time, and in the same place, the two sets of hooligans were provided with an unexpected opportunity for a fight. The police, having failed to anticipate the obvious, were nowhere to be seen. By the time they cottoned on, they were separated from the hooligans by a crowd of several hundred uninvolved supporters. The police got to the hooligans by driving right through the crowd on horseback, using their batons as they went.

I have not seen anything quite so stupid since, although I have seen many police officers compensate for their failure to control their horses by using them to push supporters up against a wall. But brutality is much more rare than simple incompetence, or overkill, or sheer inflexibility. The police gameplan determines that certain streets shall be blocked off and supporters refused access to them. Never mind if they live there, or if their cars are parked there, or that the effect is to keep supporters where they are and mix them together, rather than letting them vacate the area. But at the same time, if a street is not deemed to be their responsibility, you can be in trouble. I remember one game at the Vetch Field which was heavily policed inside the ground and in the streets precisely adjacent to the ground. Beyond that line, the police did not appear to think it was their territory. Two friends of mine were beaten up in the very next street without a policeman in sight.

Complain about there being too many police, then complain about there being too few and you appear to want it both ways at once. But the truth is that overkill and a failure to act are two sides of the same coin. The more weighed down with numbers and equipment the police are, the less able they are to think and act with flexibility. Even were that not true, it would still be unacceptable for football games to be policed as if they were national emergencies. Sometimes the police presence is out of all proportion. The critical Hereford v Brighton relegation game may have been one of the most tension-ridden games in the history of the League, but watching on the news, it was still astonishing and disturbing to see, at the final whistle, rows and rows of riot policemen charge on to the pitch, wearing helmets, carrying shields and brandishing batons.

127

There is such a thing as overkill. It is an inevitable result of seeing football as a public order problem and treating it as an exercise in saturation policing. I have seen games used as training exercises. One irrelevant end-of-season game in 1995, between Oxford and Swansea, was played on a Sunday afternoon at police insistence. This was in the era before all-day Sunday opening which, while depriving supporters of any chance to end the season by having a drink together, at the same time made the likelihood of drink-related violence absolutely minimal. Nevertheless Thames Valley Police deployed twice as many policemen as there were Swansea supporters at the game. The police declared the operation a great success. Nobody else did.

Sometimes the police appear to think that their convenience is more important than the game they are policing. They insist on rescheduling games for Sundays, on preventing games taking place at the same time as other events (a game in Scarborough was once called off due to the proximity of the Federation of Conservative Students' conference). Until a few years ago, FA Cup ties were always played to a finish, regardless of how many replays that required. This tradition ended when the police suddenly decided that they needed to be given a week and a half's notice of any replay, preventing replays taking place in the same week as the original tie. This happened even though football violence was far reduced from its level of previous years. There are not fewer police officers than there were. Though a small thing in itself, some supporters may have wondered why what had been possible 20 years ago was no longer possible in far less difficult circumstances.

Is it really harder for the police than it used to be, or have they just got too used to flexing their muscles? They should not be entitled to view football as an inconvenience. There are too many derbies already, in the North-east and South Wales, played without away fans, if not always at the explicit request of the police, then with their tacit encouragement. If football is too provocative to be played in front of two sets of supporters, there is no point in playing in the first place. That was true even in the worst days of hooliganism. It is absurd to have to make the very same point now, when ID-schemes are discredited.

But there is little sign of the policing of football easing off, becoming more tolerant. If the atmosphere in which football is played has improved, the atmosphere in political circles is harsher, less inclined to think that civil liberties are important. That is why the climate is no more favourable to the civil liberties of supporters than it was, not because of anything *we* are doing. We are seemingly subject to whatever surveillance, whatever gathering of information, the police see fit. We are filmed inside grounds and outside them, travelling to them and away from them. Sometimes fans are even stopped by the police, and made to walk towards the camera while giving their names and addresses. This sort of thing now appears to be perfectly acceptable.

While we are subject to the harsher style of the New Authoritarianism, we have been a training ground where much of it was put into practice. The atmosphere of Zero Tolerance, the style of the Criminal Justice Act, were familiar to football supporters long ago. Random searches are now provided for in law. The intrusive use of CCTV was pioneered on football supporters before it became a means of catching speeding motorists, and long before it was used for general surveillance in shopping centres and then on council estates. That is another reason why we should have been more active, more aware, in opposing police excesses in football. Those excesses are now the law for everyone. The Criminal Justice Act, in particular, can be used against supporters, not for being hooligans but for demonstrating against the owners of their clubs. Demonstrations that encroach upon the pitch, such as have taken place at many grounds in the past, can now result in imprisonment for criminal trespass.

Behaviour common, and understood, at football grounds can be construed as illegal. There is an offence of causing 'intentional harassment, alarm or distress'. If you make gestures within the sight, or address shouts within the hearing, of someone who is likely to be caused such distress, you can go to prison for six months. The clause is designed to lock up strikers who shout at scabs. But what if you shout abuse at the chairman and he demands you be arrested?

It may seem absurd, impossible that events like these could lead to imprisonment, but it is equally absurd, yet true, that laws permitting that to happen should have been passed in the first place. Sooner or later somebody will pay the penalty for it. It is absurd that it should be an offence to sell your own ticket for cost price, yet it is, and supporters have been arrested for it. It is absurd that fans should be imprisoned for travelling to a football match, yet there has already been at least one documented incident of this sort, in which Cardiff fans travelling by coach to Plymouth were stopped, searched and then locked up for seven hours. Nothing was found and nobody charged but the police were acting entirely lawfully. Things like this are happening already. The Criminal Justice Act is being used, and will be used in the future, against football supporters.

If the Criminal Justice Act can be used against us, then so can the legislation which laid some of the groundwork for the Act, the Football

Offences Act of 1991. When it went through Parliament, this Act was considered uncontroversial, discussed in terms of its clauses which allowed arrests to be made for racist chanting. These powers have remained almost entirely unused. But it also possessed clauses which made it illegal to encroach on the pitch during a game. At the time this was treated by commentators as no more than common sense.

It is no such thing. It is a potentially dangerous provision, and an unnecessary one. There are many laws that can be used, should they be necessary, against people who come on the pitch, everything from threatening behaviour to breach of the peace. There is no call for a specific law against going on the pitch itself. There is good reason to think that such a law creates more dangers than it solves.

A bad law is a law that having sought to clarify, merely makes a position less clear in the public mind. It is a law that is not enforced consistently, or cannot be. A bad law is a law that lumps together many different actions without seeking to separate them in motivation or context. This law is a bad law. The Act has not prevented people coming on the pitch. People still run on the pitch to celebrate giant-killings, to celebrate promotion or the escape from relegation. Why should they not? They mean no harm and they have been doing so for all the years that football has been in existence. Yet if they do so, police officers are quite entitled to arrest them and magistrates to punish them. What is accepted at one moment will be unacceptable at another. Supporters punished in this way are unlikely to feel that they have been treated fairly.

Being treated in an unfair manner is one thing. Being treated in a dangerous manner is another. The danger of forbidding access to the pitch is that sometimes we have to have access to the pitch. You would have thought this lesson might have been learned from Hillsborough. That disaster happened not because police officers were careless of human life but because the one thing at the forefront of their minds was that fans were not to be allowed on the pitch under any circumstances. From that presumption derived the delay in the decision to open the gates. Far from recognising that cause, and addressing it, the Football Offences Act reinforces that very preconception. In any future emergency, the same bias, against allowing supporters on the pitch, is likely to apply.

What looks like a sensible piece of legislation against bad behaviour by supporters is actually a crude assumption that football crowds can be dealt with purely as a law and order problem. That is the way in which football is normally policed. Lessons that ought to have been learned have been ignored.

Authoritarian policing always carries with it the justification that public safety, and security, is the prime objective to which all other considerations must be subordinated. In fact, public safety in football is not likely to be increased by current policing methods. This is as true of the use of surveillance and the compilation of intelligence on individuals as it is of the policing of football grounds.

The whole police intelligence-gathering operation, the existence of the National Criminal Intelligence Service Football Unit, can look like an expensive waste of time when it is asked to show results. Occasionally there is an exciting item on the news about an undercover operation. A table is prepared at Scotland Yard on which the various weapons seized are on display. But this begins to look like window-dressing when the police seem unable to anticipate organised violence. The riot in Dublin, when the Ireland-England game was abandoned due to the behaviour of England supporters, is an extremely prominent failure of police intelligence.

They had months to prepare for the game. It was a game at which it was always likely that violence, and violence involving far-right politics would occur. For many years England away matches had been a meeting place for the sort of people who were likely to organise violence at a game like Dublin. (You could hardly watch England away on television without hearing *No Surrender To The IRA*. Was that not a clue?) Yet the police were unable to act to prevent the riot. If they didn't realise it was going to happen – and everybody else did – it is hard to see how they justify their existence. But if they did know it was going to happen, but either couldn't, or didn't do anything about it, then that, too, raises the question of what they are for. Does all this expensive edifice of surveillance, of intelligence, of high-tech policing, do any more than compile a lot of information for the sake of it?

We would be better off with a great deal less of it. We ought to be realistic about this. If hooliganism is going to happen in domestic football, nobody can be expected to anticipate all of it, to prevent all of it. In fact, the more manpower is devoted to the problem, the more video footage is created, the more that the whole operation resembles an enormous, lumbering dinosaur, capable of exerting great force, but decreasingly capable of movement and thought. Everything which adds to its powers has the effect only of slowing it down further. It costs a lot of money without doing much good.

The general opinion of the effect of modern policing methods on football is that *they* are the cause of the decline in hooliganism. CCTV is given much of the credit, allowing offenders to be swiftly spotted, singled out and arrested. This proposition does not stand up to examination. If that were the case, if the *desire* to engage in violence at football games were as great as it was before, but the opportunity, *within the ground*, were much reduced, then surely that violence would only be pushed outside the ground? Wouldn't violence outside the ground be even worse than it was, rather than much reduced? The police cameras can't be everywhere. Yet that sort of violence has declined as much as violence inside the ground. Neither CCTV in particular, nor the police in general, can account for that decline.

It is more likely that football violence has simply become less attractive. It is hard to say exactly why, yet it is obvious, to everyone who has been going to football for a long time, that the *desire* to commit violence at football is much reduced. This can have nothing to do with policing methods. They can be a deterrent to violence but not a means of preventing the tendency to violence. Policing is nothing to do with it.

Perhaps it is the attritional effect of many years of public disapproval. Would-be hooligans are aware that they were making themselves extremely unpopular with fellow supporters, in much the same way that drink-driving has become a lot less common over a long period of time, because in an obvious, if indefinable manner, it has ceased to be accepted. Or perhaps Heysel convinced a lot of people that violence wasn't funny any more.

Heysel may not have bothered the most active hooligans. But for every person who actually joins in the violence there are several more who go along with it, who cheer supporters when they are led away by the police, who get excited when they talk about it. That group of people lend football violence its acceptability. They make it easier for it to happen, make it easier for new hooligans to be, as it were, recruited. They make it easier for them to convince themselves that it's all right. After Heysel, football supporters began to understand that it was very possible to end up dead at a football match. They could see that people like them had been responsible. Football violence took on a very different aura. And afterwards, however gradually, there came to be a lot less of it.

Perhaps, also, the different culture imposed on football supporters by the pressures of insecurity has changed people's minds about what it means to be a football supporter. Sacking the board is on people's minds rather than taking the end. It would be too crude to suggest that yesterday's hooligan is today's fanzine contributor. The process is far more complex than that. But we have changed quite a lot. We relate to football a bit differently from how we did before.

It is time that change was recognised in the policing of the game. We do not have to be held down by force any more. Football violence is far less prevalent now than it was ten, 20 or 30 years ago. What violence there is comes from a very small minority indeed. But we are still policed as if that violence were widespread, still subject to video surveillance, to searches, to restrictions on our movement. Is it not time that martial law was undeclared?

17. THE BEGINNING OF THE END

Football supporters mind how we are treated, but we mind even more how football is treated. Its future is as important as ours, and as insecure. The reality should not be confused with the image. New stadia and millions from television are the image. The reality, for many, is the fear of closure.

To follow football now is to live with the uneasy feeling, however far to the back of our minds we push the thought, that football is slipping slowly towards the edge. However real the threats to many clubs' existence, as long as clubs survive then their supporters have a future ahead of them. But we fear that, by one means or another, clubs will not be allowed to survive. Their future will be taken away from them. Somebody will lock the gates against football's unwanted poor and leave them to their fate, rendering their football pointless, passionless, irrelevant.

Clubs have always lived in fear of closure. That is an inevitable consequence of the economics of the game. Clubs expect to be close to bankruptcy on a semi-permanent basis. It is also a consequence of having football run by businessmen, whose natural tendency is to fear disaster at the first sign of rising overheads. Sam Hammam claims that if Wimbledon were relegated, the club would be '90-95 per cent certain' to fold. That is highly unlikely. A dozen professional clubs are relegated every year and they survive. Even Wimbledon, even shorn of television money, would survive relegation. They might sell all their players. They would cut costs. They might well slip back into obscurity. But even homeless Wimbledon would survive.

The imminence of disaster, of clubs closing all over the shop, has been predicted for so long that we have almost come to assume it can never happen. Football clubs do go out of existence, but very few, and fewer still from the ranks of professional clubs. In 50 seasons since the war, only Maidstone, Aldershot and Accrington have withdrawn from the League.

These clubs closed because of bad management (or worse) rather than any structural changes designed to starve them of their income and redistribute wealth towards the rich. That is an issue in itself – why should supporters lose their football clubs just because incompetents and fools were running them? – but these disasters were disasters particular to those clubs. That is not to be compared to what is threatened now. *Threatened* is the word. Nobody made Aldershot close. Nobody, nobody in football, wanted them to close. But there are many powerful voices in football now who do want smaller clubs to close. They want them dead. They expect them to do the decent thing. David Murray expects these clubs to hurl themselves over the edge: 'I didn't initially agree with Fergus McCann when he said there are too many clubs in Scotland. But they are basically bust some of them, and some of them must face up to that and realise it is the truth.'

He all but handed them the whisky and the pearl-handled revolver. What arrogance there is in Murray's intolerance of the smaller clubs' insistence on struggling on, rather than commit suicide at his behest. What lack of perspective he displays in believing that anyone, even himself, would benefit if smaller clubs were to be extinguished.

Murray and his mirror-image Fergus McCann are obsessed with the largely imaginary subsidies that small-town clubs in Scotland get, money which otherwise, we must assume, would be contributing to the success of Rangers and Celtic. The idea that Rangers would become a major player in Europe if only a few Brechins and East Stirlings left the stage is so absurd it barely merits saying so. But Murray and McCann can always get a hearing in the Scottish press by blaming the lower echelons of the League for Scotland's football problems.

If Brechin have a load of money stashed away which Rangers ought to have, their fans will want to know where they are hiding it. It is a nonsense. The impact on the major Scottish clubs of closing down the smaller clubs would be utterly negligible. The smaller clubs are not a weight around anybody's neck. They are simply a target on which disappointed chairmen like to take out their frustrations.

Yet the myth of the unnecessary clubs is gathering pace. As soon as Peter Leaver took office at the Premier League, he told half of the professional football clubs of England and Wales that we would be better off without them: 'My personal view is that there are probably too many clubs. I don't believe that a country like ours with a population of our size can support 92 professional football clubs. I think we must be talking somewhere between 40 and 50 full-time clubs.'

This is the same nonsense south of the border. Where does he get this concept of the population of the *country* supporting *92 clubs*? No such relationship exists. Plymouth Argyle are supported (in both senses, that of being followed and that of being financially looked after) by people who live near Plymouth or those who have Plymouth connections. They are not subsidised by people in Northumberland. The *area*, the Plymouth district, supports a full-time football club. Nor are football supporters transferable, like customers. The smaller the club, the riper for Leaver's axe, the more obviously true this is. If Plymouth closed does Leaver think thousands of Plymouth fans would go to see Torquay instead? Or Exeter? Or vice versa? If he does, then Peter Leaver knows nothing about football.

There is nothing particularly new about the idea of football being run by people who know nothing about it. Previously they were never able to do too much damage for all that. But now, the know-nothings and care-nothings have got a plan. They aim to see as many clubs closed down as they can get away with. They do not want to preserve the League. They want to cut it down. Their bias is towards seeing clubs closed rather than rescued.

That makes the prospects of struggling clubs so much bleaker. That threatens everybody. Nearly all clubs, from Hartlepool to Wolves, have at one time or another faced the threat of closure, or will, in the future face that threat. It's true that the authorities have never been too helpful to threatened clubs. While the PFA has helped out many struggling clubs with loans to get them over temporary crises, the League has never made it a point of principle to make sure that member clubs survive. They make all sorts of demands for financial guarantees, from prospective entrants in the Conference, but they make no effort to monitor the financial status of members, to prevent them getting into trouble, and they will not intervene in the running of these clubs. When things reach crisis point, their main priority is to seek guarantees that fixture lists will be completed, rather than to ask how they can help.

But they never tried to close down football clubs. 'Let them die' has never been their guiding philosophy, whereas from what Peter Leaver is saying, 'make them die' now appears to be the goal. In fact clubs do not die easily. Too many people, and too many in positions of influence in football, judge clubs' health by their financial performance rather than by the awesome fact of their survival. It is a monument to the resilience of football, and to the loyalty of its supporters, that clubs are so often in financial trouble yet so rarely succumb to their difficulties. The very fact that they survive is proof that football clubs deserve to live.

It also proves, once again, that football clubs cannot be understood as businesses, subject to business principles. If they were businesses they would certainly be closed. Football clubs survive because they are football clubs.

They can survive because they will continue to produce revenue no matter what their other difficulties are. Football clubs can guarantee a certain level of revenue. Provided they can reschedule their debts, they always have money coming in to keep them going for a little longer. The smaller the club, the smaller that income, the more likely they are to fold. But even smaller clubs, given time, patience and support, will almost always survive.

Football clubs can survive because they possess a goodwill with their creditors that other businesses do not. Creditors will accept late payment out of deference to the local community and, no doubt, to avoid losing business with that community, not wishing to be seen to be the ones who closed the local football club. Sometimes they accept no payment at all, or are prepared to walk away with almost nothing. Berwick Rangers' creditors voted to accept payment of the club's debts at nine pence in the pound, yet Berwick continued to exist. Few other businesses could write off their debts in this way.

Football clubs can survive because they provide an ever-present opportunity for good publicity. The worse the crisis, the better, and the cheaper, is that opportunity. Any businessman with cash available can rescue an ailing football club and make himself a hero. Football is cheap for some. A club looking for buyers can be picked up for next to nothing. You buy yourself a lot of goodwill and a lot of gratitude.

Football clubs almost never close. We have got used to that. That knowledge is the *only* source of confidence that fans can have when threats of closure periodically recur. But crossing our fingers may no longer be enough. It ought to be. Why should fans have to go through the trauma of fearing to lose what they hold dear? It is devastating for any fan to see their football club closed down. Even the fear of losing a football club is a nightmarish experience. Even those who have not been through it will have seen its effect on other supporters, in a series of near-closures that have run from Middlesbrough to Swansea, Bournemouth to Brighton, and many other clubs as well.

For several months in 1992 I lived with the fear that Oxford would close. Robert Maxwell died, invalidating all his guarantees that our debts would be paid. Those few months drove us frantic. The revelation of seemingly insuperable debts, the rumours, the deadlines that came and went, the expressions of interest of which nothing came, the unreality of watching games any one of which could have turned out to be our last, and so on, dragging itself out at exhausting length. We never even got to the point that Middlesbrough did of having our ground closed and chained by the Receiver, let alone to the point of Newport County, who closed down completely, the supporters left to bid for the last few relics in the grisliest of auctions.

I don't imagine Peter Leaver cares if he puts 40 or 50 sets of supporters through that sort of anguish. It would be interesting to hear him explain which clubs should be singled out for closure. Perhaps a whistlestop tour of the affected clubs could be arranged, with Leaver addressing the affected supporters and recommending which alternative clubs they might like to support. Perhaps then, people like Leaver might begin to understand. They might understand that football clubs cannot be opened up and closed down like a set of fairground stalls.

They might even understand that however unacceptable it might be from a business point of view, from the point of view of football, that dogged determination to survive is our strength. That determination gives us our longevity. With that, we have tradition, a tradition without which football would be worth nothing.

Tradition, in sport, is everything. It makes no difference how much money it can make from television. Great sporting events do not pop up overnight. They cannot be foisted on the public by any amount of hype. No event is worth anything just because it is broadcast to millions. It is only of any social significance when those millions consider it has passed the test of time.

If a new venue for Test matches was opened up tomorrow, you would have to play there for a hundred years before it even started to accumulate the gravitas that a Test at Lords possesses now. It takes many years for memories to accumulate, for records to be made and broken, for comparisons to be made. Any sporting event takes place in the shadow of its predecessors, and the longer those memories stretch into the past the more they magnify, rather than diminish, the drama of the present.

Lords has spent the last few years defacing itself with executive boxes and sponsors' logos on the outfield, but it detracts very little from the grandeur that 18 decades of cricket have bestowed upon it. Cricket knows that without its traditions it would lose its value and its depth. Sports in which the teams, the venues and the competitions change from year to year remain irredeemably shallow, no matter how spectacular they may be on television.

You can always persuade the public to watch a team that wins. *Winning* is a simple idea. It can be grasped by someone with no attachment, no understanding and no commitment. In some other sports, franchises attract enthusiastic crowds as long as they are winning, but when the winning streak ends, the crowd and the income dries up and the franchises close or move.

There have been football clubs like that, businessmen's toy teams at a non-League level. If football clubs were all like that, temporary and trivial, they would make no more claim on our imaginations than a firework display. But nearly all our clubs have been around for many decades. By that simple fact they have earned their right to their existence. By that simple fact they have created a tradition and they have given the otherwise transient events of football a depth, a social weight. Football clubs are our Lords. Darlington as well as Manchester United are our Tour de France. Leyton Orient as well as Aston Villa are our Olympics.

Why does Peter Leaver think that their supporters watch these clubs? For people to watch a club that doesn't win every week, to watch a club that sometimes hardly wins for years, they need to know that their club has been there for many years and will be there for many more. That is why football supporters are so moved by promotion or a Cup run. These are their reward for the loyalty of decades. What would football clubs be worth if they closed down when they did not succeed? That is why they matter. How often do people hold meetings and make bucket collections, donate money and shed tears, because a franchise closes down?

Of course most football clubs are bust. They always have been. So what? Closing things down because they made a loss proved a splendid way to devastate huge areas of Britain. Few of the areas concerned have seen much regenerated industry in return. It would be the same if we closed down Doncaster Rovers or Swansea City. If we reduced the number of professional clubs, no new clubs, in the same towns, would rise to replace them. This would be a slimming-down designed to let the richest grow more fat.

Leaver's is a destructive reasoning. His assumptions are the opposite of the assumptions football ought to make. How can you have too many football clubs? We still have 92 professional clubs. I wish it were 200. That may be a romantic argument. It is right nevertheless, right because it is romantic. It is also practical. The fewer clubs there are, the more they cost to watch. If we had more, the chances are that football would be cheaper. Financially cheaper, not cheaper in spirit, emptier, not like the football towards which the Murrays and the Leavers want to take us.

There is no case for closing down the smaller clubs. They hurt the interests of no other club. They provide an irreplaceable pleasure, an entertainment and a passion to hundreds of thousands of supporters. That is the argument of a football fan. It is not the sort of argument which will find favour in football's ruling circles. Football fans may feel that football clubs need to be kept alive. The ruling circles think otherwise. If it takes counsel from the more aggressive voices in the game, football may soon embark, for the first time in its history, on a deliberate, wholesale policy of closures.

How will they go about it? They cannot *order* a club to close. But they can put up obstacles, financial obstacles, of the sort that the League has recently put up to would-be entrants from the Conference, guarantees that most clubs will find impossible to give. They can turn football into a sort of private club, which only the well-off and the fortunate can possibly afford to join. They are thinking about it. It will look very businesslike indeed. It will play well with the investors in the City. But it will cut down half our football clubs, never to rise again, and with them it will cut down nine-tenths of what makes football worth a lifetime of obsession.

They may just do it. They have the power to do it and the inclination. They do not have to wait before we are persuaded in their favour. They do not need to come up with truly convincing arguments. For their sake, it is just as well, because they have none. If they think otherwise, let them produce them.

If they did, they would concentrate on business arguments and talk about the bottom line. They would have to argue that those clubs which do not make a profit cannot justify their existence, and will have to die. They would have no alternative. But nobody will be convinced. Because however skilfully they put the argument, however talented their sophistry, there is no argument on earth which can persuade football supporters that we are better off without our football clubs than with them. How would that be any sort of improvement? How are you better off when you are dead? If they think we are going to go along with that, how really stupid do they think we are?

18. FEEDING FRENZY

There is more than one way to kill a football club. You can kill it dead and leave the stadium rotting under weeds. Or you can take away its spirit and leave it like a zombie, a football club in nothing but appearance. That is exactly what they plan to do. They call it feeder status. Another term is *nursery clubs*. One club will own another. The owner club will, therefore, control the other club, its transfer policy, its team selection and its playing style. In return, they will subsidise the smaller club. It sounds like an attractive plan, provided that you know nothing about football clubs or their supporters, and care nothing either. A human being that is owned by another is a slave. A football club that is owned by another is much the same. A football club, without its independence, is not a real football club.

At the time this book was written, feeder status was not yet acceptable in football. No club may own another. No one who supports a smaller club appears to want it any other way. I have yet to meet a single fan who thinks that feeder status is an acceptable solution for whatever problems ail their clubs. You can't solve your problems by committing suicide. But if it isn't to be done by suicide, then murder must be done instead. There are many influential people within football who think that small clubs should be taken over, as if it were a kindness. I have heard the phrase 'to kill by kindness' but I have never seen it done, in football, up to now.

A lot of talks have taken place with a view to a change in rules that would allow rich clubs to swallow up their smaller brethren. All the usual suspects are involved. Alan Sugar has spoken in favour. John Hall has done the same. Doug Ellis likes it. Rick Parry has expressed the same opinion. At Sunderland, speaking in late 1996, Bob Murray made clear his interest in the change: 'We could see ourselves very much wanting to buy a nursery club. It's a very progressive thing, and the Premier League is all about progress.' By the end of the season Bob Murray had demonstrated what he understood by progress, as Sunderland progressed straight down into Division One, not least because the chairman, while quite happy to buy a club which couldn't play in the Premiership, was unprepared to buy his club some players who could. There are a lot of chairmen who think that their success makes them a guru for the rest of football. It usually turns out that they are not as visionary or as clever as they think. Some fans may fail to see why any chairman should get the chance to make a mess of two clubs instead of only one.

Nursery clubs exist in US sport, where small-town clubs, in minor leagues, are used as training grounds for the majors. Probably you have not heard of any of these nursery clubs. That is because they are nursery clubs. Obscurity is what they are designed for. US sport is nothing more than a cartel, the very sort of cartel that top Premiership chairmen would no doubt prefer to see in football. Permitting feeder status would be a large step down that road.

Everybody can see this, and if feeder status is not yet loosed upon the game one of the likely reasons is that nobody has yet thought of a way to bring it in without letting the cartel cat out of the bag. It is the first question everybody thinks of. What if a feeder team is in the same division as its owner? The potential for arranged results is obvious. It's hard enough to see how it would work if the teams were drawn together in the FA Cup. Would the feeder club try as hard as possible to eliminate their owners from the competition, thereby costing them revenue and the chance to play in Europe, or would they, accidentally and heroically, happen to lose?

In leagues such as the Spanish, where reserve teams play in lower divisions, they are not allowed to win promotion. Presumably the same, in Britain, would apply to feeder clubs. Maybe owner clubs, in order to avoid having to play their servants, would be spared the opposite, the fear of relegation? No doubt that unexpected bonus has occurred to some of the Premiership's more fertile and unprincipled minds. Either way, it's almost certain that feeder clubs would never be allowed to be promoted, not to the Premiership anyway. The dream of one day getting to the top division is what keeps these clubs alive. What would be the point of their existence then? Who will watch a team which *cannot* win, whose failure is perpetuated, till forever, by the rules? The real effect of feeder status, in this way as in many others, would be to kill these clubs stone dead.

What good is a dead club to anyone? Bob Murray claims that feeder status would allow the fans of smaller clubs to see top players play. Of course, it's not impossible to do that now. They are not so inaccessible (not yet, anyway) that we cannot see them on the television. Or, if I'm really desperate, I can save for months and buy a ticket to watch them in the Premiership (but not Bob Murray's players, not in 1997-98 at any rate). Why would I want to see these players at my local club? Barnet fans watch Barnet rather than Arsenal, not because they think they're better but because they're Barnet. If they wanted to watch Arsenal players, they would go to Highbury. Why would they go to Underhill to watch them?

Let us suppose that Arsenal did take over Barnet. What would the lucky supporters of the feeder club actually get to see? Current England and European internationals? I think not. The only way top players would turn out for a feeder side is if they were completely out of form, or injured. Or past it. Veterans are part of the entertainment in the lower divisions, showing, if they still have the attitude and application, how ability and experience can compensate for lack of speed. If all they want to do is stroll around for 90 minutes waiting for their paycheque, the fans will very quickly tell them what they think. That sort of player insults the fans who pay for him. With feeder status, fans are going to be insulted a lot more. There will be a lot more strolling around going on.

Nobody wants to pay to watch an injured player feeling their way back to full fitness, playing for half the game, playing at half-speed, avoiding all the risky bits like tackling and running, for just as long as it takes to get back to a real club that gives them real football. Professional players are not stupid. Injured or fully fit, they are hardly going to run their arses off, to risk their health and therefore their careers, playing for clubs which aren't even their real clubs.

There is a term for this. It is *reserve team football*. Football that isn't taken seriously. Anybody who knows reserve team football knows how unreal it is. No one really cares about the score. Experiments are more important than results. I've watched Oxford's reserves, but I can't imagine why, if Oxford were a feeder club, I would want to go to Oxford to watch *someone else's* reserves. Reserve games are like friendlies. It's nice to see a friendly now and then. But it is an insult to expect supporters to settle for a future where friendlies are the norm.

Feeder status is a fraud upon the public. Nothing that is said in its favour is true. We may see owner clubs farm out their younger players to give them experience. So what? They do that now. Ian Walker's professional début was for Oxford. If the promising player is at a smaller club, then even after Bosman, they are forced to pay for them. Come feeder status, they should be spared the inconvenience. Top baseball players are not seen playing in the minor leagues. Nursery sides are used to take a look at players with potential, and if they prove their worth they are not in the minor leagues for very long. The very second that a player shows potential, as soon as any player comes into form, off they will go from feeder club to owner club and not a penny will change hands.

Feeder status is not a way of letting the supporters of small clubs see good players performing for their teams. It is a way of making sure that their good players are taken away as soon as possible. It is not a way of helping smaller clubs financially. It is a way of keeping them poor and keeping them dependent.

Whose big idea is this? Where is the pressure coming from? I don't see supporters from the lower divisions agitating to be taken over by the Premiership. I do see chairmen at the top end of the Premiership, and Bob Murray, telling these supporters what is good for them. Are these chairmen the sort of individuals who are used to doing fans a favour? Are they the sort of people whose concern for smaller clubs has made them famous? Is that why they set up the Premiership? If these people want feeder status to come in, it is their own good, not anybody else's, with which they are concerned.

Why should they want to buy a feeder club? Because they have too many players and don't know what to do with them. Costly heels are being kicked for months on end. There are trophy signings who can't get a game, stockpiled youngsters to whom Premiership managers would like to give a game or two before they are forgotten, unwanted squad players who can't be got rid of before their contracts end, because no one who wants them could afford their wages.

We are expected to be very sympathetic indeed about the problems that these clubs have bought themselves. We are not. Nobody made them buy up all the players within reach, so that the shirt numbers on some teams are edging into the fifties. Why are we supposed to help them out, to give their players a game at the expense of, effectively, closing down some smaller clubs? These clubs could save themselves the trouble by buying fewer players than they do. They might allow themselves fewer mistakes. Not many managers in the Third Division get to sign a player for five million pounds, decide they've got it wrong, and get five million more to make the same mistake again. But why restrain the rich, when you can exploit the poor instead? A few clubs have acquired all the money. They have acquired all the players. Now they are asking to acquire the other clubs as well.

A small bandwagon has been getting bigger, and some cracks have started to appear in some smaller clubs' desire to retain their independence. There we have our problem. The beneficiaries of a change to feeder status are the chairmen. Chairmen of the owner clubs certainly benefit, but so do chairmen of the smaller clubs. What will appeal to these people is the fact that while the assets that they own may currently be worth almost nothing at all, if a Premiership club becomes interested in their purchase, their value will go up a long way very quickly. Some people are going to find that suddenly they are sitting on some unexpected millions. It is extremely unlikely that their fans will want them to sell out. It is also unlikely that the chairmen give a damn whether the fans want them to sell or not.

It's hard to turn down offers of free money, whether offered directly to yourself, or to the football club with whose financial situation you are struggling. Deals are starting to be made, and only the prohibition on dual ownership is going to stop one deal or another turning into full-blown feeder status. Inverness Clachnacuddin already appear to be acting as a feeder side for their League neighbours, Caledonian Thistle. At Lincoln, Fred Reames has advertised his willingness to turn his club into a nursery for anyone who wants it. Talks have been held with Newcastle. Reames is the most vocal, and the most honest, of the chairmen who would like to submerge their clubs into another. But he is unlikely to be the only one.

There is something called an 'alliance' between Liverpool and Crewe. Nobody outside the boardroom knows exactly what that means. Crewe fans asked their board, at open meetings, what it meant, and were directed to look it up in the dictionary. An alliance. In practice it certainly meant that one Crewe hopeful trained at Anfield rather than Gresty Road, at a time when Crewe were fighting for promotion. Arrangements like those may seem to be of mutual benefit from the perspective of the boardroom, but for supporters they have a different meaning altogether. They are not trusted. They look like the thin end of the wedge.

Oxford were reported to be trying to sell themselves, in one way or another, to Juventus. According to the local papers, this meant young Italians getting experience in England. According to the *Sun*, it meant Alessandro Del Piero in an Oxford shirt. Nobody who knew the truth was telling anyone who didn't. It did, however, seem obvious to anyone who thought about it that if a club of Juventus' size bought a stake in one like Oxford, they were doing so for their own benefit and that in any conflict of interest, the more powerful party was more likely to prevail. Being a vassal of Juventus held very little appeal to this Oxford supporter.

From the start of the 1997–98 season, Football League clubs were permitted to take two under-23 players each on loan for an entire season. The idea was that big Premiership clubs would be able to give their players extended experience at a professional level. The idea was promoted as beneficial to both parties. But the flaws, the dangers, were evident. Who would pull the strings? Would smaller clubs be able to drop players they didn't fancy, or would they be expected to do the larger club's bidding? Whatever the rules, in football money is power and money talks. And every change in football's structure is a step towards a larger change. This was a move towards feeder status, opening the door that little bit wider, and was, therefore, a move to be deplored.

None of these proposals, none of these arrangements has yet transformed itself into feeder status, but they all mean that the danger is approaching ever closer. Just as we are expected to dismantle the domestic competitions to suit the requirements of the richer clubs, and never mind the needs of the smaller, so we are now expected to dismantle the smaller clubs themselves. This is no sort of solution for smaller clubs, it is not 'realistic', it is nothing but their extinction. Feeder status is not going to revitalise interest in any football club. It will only diminish it. A feeder club will be a kept club, a joke club, a club that nobody takes seriously.

The Morlocks are coming for the Eloi. All the Morlocks need now is for football to give up quietly. That doesn't have to happen. Nothing has to happen. The FA do not ever have to change their rules. They do not have to do everything that John Hall tells them to. But they have never yet stood up to him. They couldn't even stand up to Bill Archer. If these are all that stands between a football club and nemesis, then God alone can help that football club.

The fans, of course, are not so pliable. But we have no official say. We have the power to oppose but not the power to determine, and if we can be fooled, even for just a short time, with promises of top players and lies about retaining independence, then possibly our guard will drop as well. They only have to get away with feeder status once and then the floodgates may begin to open.

Feeder status is as insidious an idea as anything in football. It offers money as a smokescreen, with the idea of taking it away. It offers us survival at the price of taking away independence. Nobody can honestly support it who would not accept it for their own club, and nobody would. Nobody wants their football club to be killed off. This is what this is. Feeder status is not a solution. It is an execution.

19. TWO CLUBS ARE BETTER THAN ONE

Force football clubs to dance to the tune of maximum profitability and sooner or later you will force some of them to close. Treat them as business opportunities and sooner or later you will see them close anyway. A lot of money can be made running football clubs. A lot of money can also be made closing football clubs. You can make that money by selling their grounds for property development. You don't even have to be doing it for personal profit. You can be doing it as a short-term fix to raise the money to pay off a debt. But whether the profit be for personal use or not, the danger is the same. A club that sells its ground without a new one is a club in danger of closing down.

A second danger is that a club may be merged with another club. It is related to the first, because the basic motive for the merger, whatever is claimed about building a stronger club, is likely to be the financial opportunity provided by one of the clubs vacating its ground and freeing it for sale. Related also because such mergers would be impossible if it were not accepted that football clubs are the property, morally as well as legally, of those who own them, theirs to do with as they please. If football clubs were institutions, not merely property, if those who owned them were custodians and were not free to dispose of that property as they pleased, then the security of football clubs would be totally different from the current, precarious position.

A third danger is of clubs moving, from one town to another town entirely, transplanted by an owner looking for more commercially fertile soil for the future. Supporters run the risk of being left bereft, of having their club removed and renamed, without consent or consultation. The

147

number of clubs at risk of removal right now may be small, as indeed is the number who may face merger or closure in one way or another. But that risk is growing and supporters of no small club can be sure they are safe.

Risks to football clubs are like risks to the environment. They almost always lie in the future, often a long way in the future. The risks themselves are unpredictable. But we know for certain that if we take no notice, when we see the first symptoms of a problem, we run the risk of encountering disaster when it will be too late to act. Football supporters can never be too aware, too well informed, too careful about what may be in store for us. The risks are real and they are real now.

The idea of merger crops up in football every so often, every few years. Usually it never quite happens. In 1982 Robert Maxwell announced his bizarre and abortive Thames Valley Royals scheme, in which he proposed to merge Oxford and Reading. The plan was for the new club to play alternately at the Manor and Elm Park, until a new stadium could be built in Didcot, midway between the two. Fans who opposed the plan were rebuked for their 'parochialism' and 'conservatism'.

Five years later, David Bulstrode, then owner of QPR, proposed to close Fulham, whom he temporarily controlled as well. He planned their incorporation into QPR. The press nicknamed the new club Fulham Park Rangers. At much the same time, Ron Noades had a plan to close down Wimbledon and merge it into Crystal Palace, something that Wimbledon fans had not forgotten, about which they were still nervous, when Wimbledon sold Plough Lane and moved into Selhurst Park.

None of these clubs were minnows, unable to survive independently, unable to achieve success in their existing form. Wimbledon were already in the old First Division, only one season away from winning the FA Cup. Fans may assume that only lame ducks, only very small, mostly unnoticed clubs are at risk of merger, that if they support a club that is currently doing well, that has a decent level of support, then nobody can touch them. Not so. When merger next reared its ugly head, in Scotland, one of the oldest and most famous clubs in the country, Hibernian, was the intended sacrifice. Wallace Mercer, chairman of Hearts, intended to merge the two, or rather, to close down Hibernian and transfer their players and assets to Hearts.

All these mergers failed. None of them failed because the press campaigned against them, thereby turning public opinion against the agents of merger. Much of the press supported Mercer, seeing him as a visionary, seeing nothing wrong with killing off a football club with a century of history behind it. Fulham Park Rangers was reported as a *fait accompli*, as if, once a chairman had handed down a decision, that was the end of that. Football supporters are not so fatalistic, or so pliable. Every last one of the mergers was killed by opposition from supporters.

Robert Maxwell is long gone but Oxford and Reading are still with us. There were marches, public meetings, pitch invasions and centre-circle sit-ins. It took only two months for the supporters' parochialism and conservatism to triumph, despite all Maxwell's wealth, power and influence.

Fulham Park Rangers succumbed to the antagonism of supporters and the opposition of Hammersmith and Fulham District Council which, combined, forced the Football League into making Bulstrode relinquish control of Fulham. At Selhurst Park, Palace supporters were actually permitted to vote on merger, a referendum which, despite asking a loaded question designed to elicit a vote of YES to merger, obtained a NO majority of nearly 12 to one. Ron Noades summed up his attitude to supporters with his customary tact and sympathy: 'That's an indication of the intelligence of the average football supporter. I only hope when they fill in the form they can write.'

Supporters can do rather more than merely write. They can frustrate the megalomania of football chairmen. Fans killed the Hearts merger as well. Led by Hibs fans, but enthusiastically supported by supporters of many other clubs, including Hearts themselves, a Hands Off Hibs campaign preserved Hibernian's independence. Unlike Maxwell and Bulstrode, Wallace Mercer is still alive, but he, too, is long gone from football. Hibernian, and their supporters, are still there. That tells you all you need to know about these mergers. They are presented as the best hope, sometimes the only hope for these clubs, protecting the real interests of supporters. The supporters almost always oppose them. It inevitably turns out that they know better. Oxford were such dead ducks in 1982, so incapable of progressing on their own, that within three years they were in the top division, and one year later won the League Cup. Reading have survived and had their share of success. Chairmen cry wolf, prophesy disaster if their proposals are rejected, when what they really mean is that they've been caught doing what they should not be doing. That is what mergers are about.

Supporters might have thought that after so many high-profile victories over the chairmen the concept of merger might have been laid to rest. When the spectre appeared again it was in rugby league. Among Rupert Murdoch's requirements for the creation of Super League were several mergers designed to ensure that only one club was allowed to exist in any one area covered by the League. Among the mergers demanded were the merger of Widnes and Warrington and that of Castleford and Featherstone. Rough equivalents in football might be the merger of Birmingham and Aston Villa and that of Southampton and Portsmouth. Again, the supporters would not accept it, although it was approved by the rugby league authorities and much of the press. Again, they campaigned hard against each merger and again they were right. Again, they won. Sky TV backed off. None of these clubs were closed.

Wherever major mergers are proposed, they seem to be defeated. Yet sometimes, on a smaller scale, they are not. Rushden and Diamonds were formed from a merger of Rushden Town and Irthlingborough Diamonds. In Inverness, Caledonian merged with Thistle. They actually balloted fans beforehand but on the understanding that only if the clubs agreed to merge would they be permitted to join the League. Even then the results of the ballot remain disputed. But Inverness Caledonian Thistle are a reality.

These are not, except to their supporters, clubs of great significance. But one merged club is playing in the Scottish League, and the other has ambitions on the Football League. Put it that way and it becomes a little more significant. The precedent has been set. The wall has been breached. They know that they can get away with it.

In the case of Inverness at least, the consideration of the value of empty property does not appear to have been a major influence on the decision. Nor in rugby league, in which sport Rupert Murdoch was trying to create a tailor-made league for television purposes. Maxwell's Didcot plan was probably the product of nothing more than an ego, a whim and a failure to understand what football was about. But where Maxwell may have been driven by nothing more rational than megalomania, Bulstrode and Noades were acting at a time when property prices, especially in London, were reaching impossible heights. Plough Lane and Craven Cottage, emptied of their football teams, would have been worth a lot of money. Even after the bursting of the property bubble, the same may be true of Easter Road, if liberated from Hibernian. Property is still bought and sold. Even now, football grounds, as any Brighton fan can tell you, are still available for sale.

Chairmen are not less avaricious than they were ten years ago. Restrictions on cross-club ownership are not more effectively policed. Are the football authorities, even if they possessed the backbone or the will to act, capable of resisting the brute force of finance? One doubts it. It is easy to see how any property developer might look at Stoke and Port Vale, or at the two adjacent clubs in Dundee, and decide that one of them was surplus to requirements, sitting on a site crying out for development.

If we can see that, we see it as a danger. There will be those who see it just as well, but see it as an opportunity. I can imagine them looking at Walsall, at Leyton Orient, at Rochdale and considering their survival an unnecessary anomaly, their ground an unnecessary expense. A groundshare – with whom makes little difference – would follow from the sale of the ground. It would make tremendous business sense, would rationalise, cut costs. In football there is always one easy way to cut your costs. You manage it by stopping football being played.

Following the likely decline in support and crowd receipts, the likely outcome would be an attempt at closure or merger, if there is any difference between the two. A merger is a closure. We watch our clubs because they are our clubs. You cannot half-support a club that's only half your club. (What are you going to do? Cheer just the attack? Or just the defence? Support only the players who came from *your* club? Support them only at the weekend? Or only in midweek?)

The fallacious idea is that a merged club combines the support of both teams that preceded it. As that combined support propels the club to greater heights, it will pick up more support in addition. It may work like that while they're winning, spending the money gained from flogging off the dead club's assets. But when the novelty wears off and the casual fans go home, nothing is left. No sense of history, identity or pride, none of the things that keep us going through the gates in normal circumstances. The long-term consequences of a merger will be a lot of money in the chairman's pocket and a nothing team playing nothing football for nearly nobody.

At least you cannot merge a football with a rugby team, which makes the QPR groundshare with Wasps, whatever the financial motives, reasonably safe, for QPR at least. But in Scotland, groundshares have become more common. Hamilton sold their ground with so little foresight that the chairman who sold it left for Falkirk before a new ground was on the horizon. Hamilton lodge at Albion Rovers. Airdrie share with Clyde. Clydebank, having, like Hamilton, sold their ground without getting a new one, are living at Dumbarton without, at time of writing, any apparent clue what they are going to do for another ground. This sort of thing makes supporters nervous. Mergers are not always on the cards but closures are entirely possible.

When they are torn away from their roots, unless supporters have a clear idea of how, and when, they are going to get home, they fear for the future. They fear that a club without a home will eventually cease to be a club. They feel insecure. What has lost its permanent home can easily become impermanent itself.

Manchester United or Juventus might be able to dispense with their roots. Most clubs cannot. Every game that Bristol Rovers played at Twerton Park, that Charlton played at Selhurst Park or Upton Park, was a game played in alien surroundings. The distance from Bristol to Bath is only a dozen miles. The average supporter's journey to Stamford Bridge or Old Trafford is probably rather further. But Rovers supporters were travelling *away* from their home, not towards it. The feeling of insecurity and rootlessness was palpable.

Charlton supporters went to the lengths of standing in elections against hostile councillors to prove that neither they, nor their club, were unwanted in the borough they belonged in. Without that campaign, Charlton would not, today, be playing at the Valley. They might not be playing anywhere at all. It would be so easy for clubs like these to fade away. When they do not have a ground to call their own, their support begins to dwindle, their ability to raise funds for a new ground correspondingly diminishes, as does the hope of ever finding one. Football clubs do not die easily but making them homeless does not do a great deal for their health.

It is folly to move a football club from town to town. It only gives the directors ideas. They start thinking of ways to move the club to somewhere more suitable. More suitable for them, not more suitable for the supporters. Of course it is true that many clubs, at one time or another, have moved from one site to another, even a club of the stature of Arsenal, who moved from Woolwich, in South-east London, to Highbury, in North London, before the First World War. Yet most moves of this sort were made before football clubs acquired any real history, before their roots were sunk too deep. After many decades of existence, you cannot transplant a football team as easily as that.

Moves of any distance are extremely rare. They are more often planned than carried out. In 1965 East Stirling moved to Clydebank, only to have a judge decide that the move was illegal and make them move back. David Evans wanted to move Luton to Milton Keynes. Southend planned a move to Basildon and banned a number of opponents of the move from Roots Hall. But Luton are still in Luton, Southend in Southend. East Stirling are still in Falkirk. Just as with the mergers, the fans have mostly defeated these schemes. But there have been defeats as well. Meadowbank, with the complicity of the Scottish League, were whisked away up the M8, from Edinburgh to Livingston, and renamed Livingston Thistle.

That is not the same club under a different name and at a different location. It is a new club. Meadowbank Thistle have been destroyed. That is a threat which still hangs over Wimbledon, who have considered moving house to Dublin, or a move to Basingstoke. Wimbledon fans can easily be deprived of their football club. The supporters would be devastated. The club itself would be no more.

There is no reason why Dublin, or Basingstoke, or anywhere, should not play host to a prominent and successful football club. There is no reason why Livingston should not have a club playing in the Scottish League. Provided, in each case, that it is a club of their own. Meadowbank were not Livingston's to have. Wimbledon are for Wimbledon supporters, not for fans in Basingstoke or Dublin.

Anybody who wants to set up a new club in any of these places has every right to do so. But they do not have the right to cut corners by taking away somebody else's club. The principle is the important thing, the principle that says that football clubs are the moral property of their supporters. Chairmen complain about the terrible difficulties they have in making clubs a paying proposition. There is a simple answer to those chairmen. If they find it too difficult, they always have the option to get out. No matter what their contribution, no matter who they are, be they Sam Hammam or anybody, nobody is insisting that they stay in the game.

Football is not a blank sheet of paper on which anything the chairmen want can be inscribed. Football clubs and their history are not to be disposed of in this way. It doesn't matter how economically irrational some clubs' locations may appear to be. What is wrong with having small professional football clubs? Small clubs don't need to move somewhere to find a bigger audience. They need to stay exactly where they are. It doesn't matter if there are two teams in Nottingham, two in Bristol, two in Falkirk, two in Stoke. These little quirks and anomalies are part of our fabric and our history. And only a philistine treats history as disposable.

The will of supporters is always to remain on their home territory. The will of supporters is almost always against merger. Nothing lasting, nothing of value, can be achieved against the will of the supporters. Supporters and their clubs are the only fixed points of reference in football. Everything else changes and only we, and they, remain. They are trying to change that if they can. They are already quite prepared to get rid of some of the supporters. They are prepared to get rid of some of our football clubs. We have learned in the past that we can stop them. We are going to have to remember that lesson in the future. We have everything to lose if we do not.

20. SIGNIFICANCE

Nothing can be good for football supporters if it damages the interests of the clubs they follow. To the supporter this may be obvious. But it is usually forgotten by those who are excessively impressed by the top end of the Premiership, by the international stars on *Match Of The Day*. They forget that this really doesn't matter to supporters whose clubs aren't on *Match Of The Day*. It is nice to have top players to watch. Everyone enjoys seeing the game played by its most highly skilled exponents. But unless it happens at your club, it is peripheral to what's really important.

The universe revolves round whatever club we happen to follow, whether it be Manchester United or Mansfield. We understand that what happens elsewhere in football is important, but it is not worth losing what we have just so that some other clubs can employ some world-class players. It is not a fair exchange. It is taking away what matters to us and giving us something that really doesn't matter at all. The superstars are an optional extra. They are part of the entertainment. But they are not what's really important in the game.

What matters is what happens to our football clubs. Football is football clubs. What is the first question you ask another supporter? *Who do you support?* We are our football clubs. We refer to them as *us* and *we*, we live the game through their success and failure. Of course it is an absurd relationship. But there is no point in complaining about it. That is the way it is, that is what happens, and until society adopts more civilised forms of living, we will continue to live through football in the way that we do now. We are our football clubs. Our aspirations in the game are the aspirations of those clubs.

That is the rhythm of football from top to bottom. It doesn't matter very much what those particular aspirations are. Everything is just another step on the same ladder, promotion from the Third Division no less important than promotion from the Second, each of them another step towards the highest level you can go. Everyone aspires to different things but everyone aspires in the same way. All professional football clubs, and all clubs who aspire to be professional, are in an important sense the same. The desire to climb is the same among the foothills as it is towards the summit.

Everything is possible. For football to mean anything, it must be possible. Football generates hope as often as it produces despair. That hope is always there. Every relegation can be reversed. Every late equaliser, every step up the table, every small, fleeting moment of unexpected skill is a renewal. Stay up, stay up and next year hopes are for promotion. The long march begins again.

Everything is possible. Leyton Orient played a solitary season in the First Division. So did Northampton Town and so did Carlisle United. One season, Rotherham missed that opportunity only on goal difference. All of these are clubs who are either in the Third Division or were promoted from it while I was writing this book. Their motivation is their potential for the future. The proof of that potential is their past. All of them have a history that provides them and their supporters with the knowledge that it is worth it.

It only took Wimbledon nine seasons of League football to reach the promised land. Oxford did it in 23. Barnsley supporters waited 98 years. Reading have yet to make it, although they have played League football for nearly 80 years. In 1995 they led the play-off final, missing a penalty at two-nil up, before the prize slipped from their grasp. These clubs make every other club worthwhile. They make it impossible to honestly dismiss the lower divisions. The struggle to stay among the élite may be ultimately futile, but the struggle to get there is not.

Non-league clubs aspire to one day join the League. Professional clubs set their sights on the top division. Top division clubs aim at success in Europe and the Championship. Everybody has something to play for. Without that, football is sterile. But the most powerful voices in football do not understand that hope. They do not need it and they do not want it. What they want is to hang on to what they've got. And they have already learned, from the experience of creating the Premiership and the Champions' League that if the structure of football doesn't suit you, you can change it.

This is yet another way in which they can kill our football clubs and kill, with them, our pleasure and our interest in the game. You can kill them by depriving them of the hope of better things to come. The very structure of football, the promotion and relegation which are integral to its drama, is a threat to the financial ambitions of those who have a lot of money riding on it. Sport thrives on risk. But money thrives on the lack of it. The greater the financial stake in football, the greater the incentive of those who own and control that stake to try and reduce those risks to a minimum. Promotion and relegation, and the latter in particular, are the whole point of football for supporters. We cannot imagine the game without them. But there are certainly influential people in the game who, one way or another, are trying to imagine just that.

There is nothing more guaranteed to bring about an attack of narrow vision than the fear of financial loss. You can argue that football will be more profitable in the long term if the risks of relegation are retained, because it will be more exciting, because clubs who are willing to spend will replace those who are not. This might even be true. But the long-term future of football is not what occupies the minds of chairmen whose clubs hover above the Premiership relegation zone, whose shares tumble in value, whose thoughts revolve round television money and its imminent disappearance. They do not think about the grim fascination that the threat of relegation lends to football. They think about how it could be avoided.

What these people think about is reconstruction. Their model league would not be the English or the Scottish version, either of them leagues in which there is a very long way to fall. It would be the National Football League, in which there is nowhere to fall and every landing is a soft one. They would probably like a league which was entirely self-contained, just as the League once was before automatic promotion from the Conference, when admission to the League was theoretically possible but usually, in practice, didn't happen. Clubs at the bottom of the Fourth Division didn't have much, but at least they had security. Chairmen of leading clubs envy them that, if nothing else.

There is no masterplan, no conspiracy (not yet, anyway) but there are a number of signs that chairmen are not happy with the situation they are in, and that they would like to change it. There is a permanent discussion of the possibility of reconstruction and a disturbing amount of thinking the unthinkable is going on. Some chairmen are willing to think it aloud. The Scottish magazine *The Absolute Game* carried a highly revealing interview with the chairman of Hearts, Chris Robinson, revealing not just for what it said, but for the fact that a leading chairman was prepared to say it in the presence of a fanzine. Time was when influential people planned their breakaways behind our backs but now the movers and shakers are sufficiently confident that they can tell us to our faces what they want to do.

Robinson explains why Scottish Premier League clubs have toyed with reconstruction. His language tells us as much about his ideas as do those ideas themselves. 'A number of Premier clubs had invested a lot of money and were expressing common concerns at that time about how the league structure was placing pressure upon these investments. Everybody knows the effect that being outwith the Premier League has on a club's finances . . . ultimately the larger full-time clubs are going to demand more insurance.'

The *league structure* places *pressure* on *investments*. Relegation might cost us money and should therefore be prevented. *Insurance.* No danger. No acknowledgement that if you want to enjoy the benefits of success you should also accept the risks of failure. Insurance is too generous a term. Insurance is compensation when something goes wrong, but for Robinson the whole idea is to stop things going wrong at all.

Forget your drama, forget your romance. The top division would be filled not by footballing merit but by appointment, and only the powerful and profitable would come into consideration: 'I think there will be more pressure for membership of the Premier League to become subject to certain criteria on stadium facilities and the ability to fill those stadiums. If you look at the demographics you'd also have to say there should be one team from Ayrshire, one from Lanarkshire, Fife, Tayside and so on.'

The Absolute Game: 'You're surely not advocating amalgamations?'

'No. I'm simply suggesting that in those areas you would ideally select the strongest and best supported side for membership of the top league.'

You would *select* a side for membership. *Select.* Let Raith come top of the First Division all they like, if they hadn't got the crowd figures and the television audience to show for it, they would stay exactly as they were. Their supporters could get stuffed. It isn't a question of being unfair to a football club, a company. It would be the supporters who were cheated, cheated of their money, cheated of their dreams, cheated of their commitment.

It would be Keighley all over again. Points would be no match for profit margins and population figures. That is the vista which people like Chris Robinson look forward to. Football would be a world of barren certainties. That is the price of football clubs' insurance.

Of course, Robinson was reporting proposals which had not come to fruition. The discussions had not led to a conclusion. There is no franchise system hanging over Scottish or English football at the moment. But that is no guarantee it will not happen in the future. Robinson has told us, after all, that such things are being discussed. If they have gone cold for the minute, they can be heated up later. The Premiership breakaway was discussed in various forms and defeated several times before it actually came to pass. If plans like these are being discussed now, the only certainty is that they are not going to go away. Rather than being reassured about the situation, we ought to be extremely disturbed that these ideas are discussed at all.

Reconstruction of one sort or another, always in the direction of less free access to the top division, *is* under discussion in both Leagues, in Europe and lower down the Football League. The Premiership has held discussions with the Football League with a view to reducing the number of relegation places from three to two. The League may seem unlikely to agree ('We're making loads of money up here compared to you, how would you like to reduce your chances of getting some?') but the question is not being asked for no reason. The reasons for asking it are not going to go away.

Cut relegation to two a season? Why as many as that? The Premiership has got the power to make its own decisions. It has the power to ignore the League if it thinks it necessary. Eventually it may well use that power to preserve itself from the ugly consequences of its own system. The same question is being posed at several different levels within the game. The owners of a number of middle-sized clubs, concerned about their inability to compete with the Premiership, afraid of falling back into the lower divisions, would like to make sure that a line is drawn between them and their lower-ranked colleagues in the League.

There has already been at least one attempt to create a second Premiership, to cut the League in two and dispose of the lower half, in a way Peter Leaver might approve of. (More than one if we include the abortive 'Phoenix League' that was floated in summer 1997.) In 1995 the then chairmen of Norwich, Crystal Palace and Oldham, Robert Chase, Ron Noades and Ian Stott, used a dispute over the division of television income to threaten a breakaway division and to invite the rest of the First Division to join them.

The detail of the proposal never became clear, partly because it had not been prepared properly, partly because they failed, narrowly, to gain enough support. But it was clear that television money was only the smokescreen for other concerns. The First Division already kept the lion's share of the television money. What was left was hardly worth arguing over, let alone setting up a whole new league. Nor was there any encouragement from above. The Premiership was far too keen to keep its money to itself to contemplate taking a new breakaway under its wing.

If there wasn't much money to be gained by a breakaway, all that could have remained, by way of motive, was to offer middle-ranking clubs some degree of control over their own destiny which they did not currently have. A breakaway could be sold as a means of sealing off the First Division at the lower end, and guaranteeing that no club would slip, as Oldham subsequently did, into the abyss of Divisions Two and Three. It might be a closed division or it might not, but any admission could be restricted, if required, to appointment only. Nobody actually said so. But what else could they possibly have been driving at? Stott, Noades and Chase had all been in the Premiership at its inception. They had expected to be dining at the trough and had been elbowed out. They did not want the risk of missing out again.

Clubs will no longer tolerate the risk of losing. Clubs in the First Division do not wish to contemplate being more than one step away from the Premiership. Clubs who flirt with relegation from the Premiership do not want to lose their television money. Nor do clubs who expect to play in Europe. At the very top end of the scale, some of these clubs expect to do to Europe what Chris Robinson only dreams of doing for Scotland, and create a self-selecting league. Already the creation of the monstrous Champions' League shows what damage rich club owners will do to football's integrity, if they think they can, thereby, increase and safeguard their profits.

The European Cup was one of the greatest, most prestigious football competitions in existence. It owed that prestige to the fairness and simplicity of its format, not to the money it could potentially produce. Every country, regardless of size, had one participant, who had to be the national champions. The Cup format allowed no second chances for clubs who made mistakes. It was a classic competition. But these very characteristics which made it great were characteristics with which the richest clubs could not be comfortable.

You couldn't let just anyone join in. When the Cup first became the League, the champions of smaller, poorer countries were excluded from the competition. You couldn't have equal chances for everyone when television companies were paying good money to follow English, German and Italian clubs. So the structure of the competition was changed so that clubs from richer, more successful countries were seeded beyond the knockout stages. You could not let these clubs be knocked out just because they lost. In 1996-97 Manchester United contrived to reach the semi-final, despite losing five matches on the way, which would have been almost impossible when it was a real cup. Nor could you let powerful clubs, who might have invested a lot of money trying to win their national league, miss out just because they only came second. So some richer countries, like England, were permitted to enter a second club in the Champions' League. Clubs who were, by definition, not the champions. At that point the Champions' League finally ceased to be a game of football and became a means of waving money in the public's face.

To protect clubs who did not need protection, the European Cup was robbed of all the charm that it possessed. The UEFA Cup was mangled. Each was a step towards the European League which is the goal of Milan, Juventus, Barcelona and Manchester United. Any number of formats for that league have been discussed. But we can be certain that the initial format will not be permanent and that whatever changes are then made, they will reduce access for the outsiders and increase security for the European élite. The very creation of the European League will produce television revenue of such proportions that those who share in it are not going to accept the risk of losing it.

The Italian politician and owner of Milan, Silvino Berlusconi, commissioned the football analyst and consultant Alex Fynn to come up with some proposals. The proposals he produced were not to Berlusconi's satisfaction. Too much was left to chance. Fynn comments: 'I believe in merit and chance and one of the things Berlusconi said which turned me off him was that the European Cup was totally against modern business thinking. I soon realised that what I'd done was really wrong.'

Fynn was also the author of the *Blueprint For Football* which launched the Premier League which, he also later realised, has done untold damage to the financial structure of English football. Still, there is more joy in heaven at one sinner who repenteth . . . and Fynn is a useful witness because Berlusconi has enormous influence and no one is better placed than Fynn to understand what Berlusconi wants. He comments: 'What someone like Berlusconi really wants is a franchise system and even under the current set-up, Rosenberg can knock Milan out which none of the big clubs want.'

Or Galatasaray can knock out Manchester United. These clubs expect their place on the gravy train to be reserved, and theirs is to be a first-class carriage, year after year. That is the sort of arrangement 'modern business thinking' wants to see. Losing football games must not be allowed to make a difference to the final results. And if losing no longer makes a difference, if it doesn't matter, then football no longer matters. In which case, it is dead.

Scottish football discusses a closed Premier League. English football discusses limiting promotion to the Premiership and to the First Division. European football moves towards automatic qualification to the Champions' League and beyond that, towards some sort of franchise system. That is the way the wind is blowing. We move towards the edge. Every new proposal for reconstruction is designed to smother what life is left in football, and in smaller clubs especially. If it is not the Premiership it is the threat of feeder clubs. If it is not a second Premiership it is the threat of regional and, sooner or later, part-time football.

Reconstruction can be used to lock the smaller clubs out of the Premiership. It can also be used to make the football that they play less compelling, less consequential, not because they are deprived of their aspirations for the future but because the football they play in the present is downgraded. In the face of crisis there is a tendency to thrash about for gimmicks and quick fixes. The League commissioned the Deloitte and Touche report, which proposed that the lower divisions be split up into North and South, just as they were before the Fourth Division was set up in 1958, because small clubs pay out a lot in travelling expenses. With all the usual confidence of the ill-informed, they simply proposed to bring the old regional Third Division back again, and by that means, to cut costs.

You could do that. But afterwards you'd have to cut again, and a great deal more deeply as well, because nobody would want to watch regional football. The fans can tell the difference between football that we can take seriously and football that we can't. We know that friendlies do not matter. We know that relegation does. We know that testimonials, that end-of-season games, that early rounds of the Auto Windscreens Shield, that games between reserve teams, in various different ways, are never to be taken seriously because they do not take themselves seriously. Significance is everything.

If football downgrades itself, if it decides that it can no longer sustain a national division, if clubs no longer want to pay for full-time professionals, then football says it is not important. It says that football clubs are *not* the same, that there is real football only at the top, and far below, there is half-real football, clubs playing in a half-division, employing players who are half-professionals. Regional football would not be half as significant as football in a national league. It would be lucky to attract half as big a crowd.

Significance is everything. The only way to make the game significant, to make small town football matter, is to go in exactly the opposite direction from the way prevailing trends would have us go. It is to maintain national divisions, not split them up. It is to increase relegation and promotion, not abandon them. It works. The real success of English football over the last decade is not the Premiership. It is not the festival of greed, but the revitalisation of the grassroots. The real success has been the Conference.

Rather than split football into regional divisions, the Conference welded them together. Rather than cut clubs off from promotion, it secured an automatic promotion place which it did not have before. Non-league football was transformed. Crowd figures rose by far greater percentages than the Premiership has managed. As 1986-87, the first season of automatic promotion, drew to a close with Scarborough edging out Kettering and Barnet, the media, for whom non-League football had previously not existed, began to take note of the drama. There was live commentary on Burnley's emotional escape from relegation. Live commentary, from the wrong end of Division Four.

By 1997 interest and awareness had risen to a level where 6,000 fans could pack into Broadhall Way three months before the end of the season to see Stevenage play Kidderminster. Eight thousand saw Yeovil play Enfield, not even in the Conference but in the league below. These are fantastic crowd figures for non-League football. They show the depths of public interest which previously insignificant clubs could wake among the public, if only they took themselves as seriously as their fans take them. Revitalising non-League football did the League no harm either. Clubs like Burnley and Tranmere were ultimately beneficiaries of their own brush with disaster. The bottom of the League was able to take on such significance that few Premiership games in 1996-97 commanded the column inches, or the public interest, that were provoked by the final match between Brighton and Hereford.

That is a lesson, if football would only learn it. You gain nothing by letting yourself be downgraded. All you do is prevent yourself being taken seriously. All that transpires is that the rich and greedy get everything they want. For years, the main body of football accepted anything the élite clubs demanded, making each concession in order to stave off the direst threats of breakaways, each concession only encouraging the élite to come back for more. Finally it has filtered through to some of the club chairmen that it is time to change their tactics.

At some of the smaller clubs, the owners have apparently decided that they are not going to roll over and die quietly. No doubt they are acting in self-interest, but despite that, and despite whatever other deficiencies they may possess, some chairmen have played a small but vital part in holding back the tide. Jack Steedman, at Clydebank, has responded to the plottings of élite club chairmen by threatening to propose a reconstruction that, increasing the size of the top division, would suit the smaller clubs. He has organised conspiratorial meetings of his own from which the élite chairmen were excluded. If nothing else, it serves as a warning shot across the bows.

In England, Fred Reames of Lincoln, with Geoffrey Richmond of Bradford, worked hard and agitated among other chairmen to fight off Stott, Chase and Noades. Reames proceeded to help kill off the Deloitte and Touche report. For the moment, regionalisation is dead.

Steedman it was who tried to move East Stirling to Clydebank. Reames is an advocate of feeder status. Richmond dumped Scarborough because Bradford were a more promising prospect. None of these people's loyalty to football can be relied on. But nevertheless, there is a real struggle going on in football, and however one-sided it is in terms of economics, it is not a struggle that football, or supporters, are doomed, in advance, to lose.

It is a struggle for significance, and it affects more clubs and more supporters than they may realise. It affects supporters of clubs outside the League but also those outside the First Division, those outside the Premiership and even those outside the top two of the country. It doesn't matter exactly what you aspire to, the important thing is to aspire. Supporters of Leeds, of Chelsea, of Aston Villa aspire to see their clubs compete in Europe. When there is a European League, they would expect their clubs to have the chance to play in it, and if they find themselves excluded, if they are prevented from having the chance to rise to that level, then they, too, will feel their football shrunken in significance, lifeless, lacking satisfaction.

Sterile football towards the top and lifeless football at the bottom. That is the direction in which we are going. Let the Stotts, the Robinsons and the Berlusconis have their way, and that is what we will be left with. Football, at any level, thrives when, and only when, it begins to matter. That is what makes the game compelling. That is what we have to preserve. That thread of mutual interests links supporters from the highest of clubs down to the lowest, and it links us together against those who see football as their honeypot, and against those who seek to shape it purely for their own convenience. Once again, it is us against them.

21. THE HEALTH OF THE COMMUNITY

It is not the nature of profit to moderate its thirst for more. As so much profit is being made, we must assume that current trends in football are going to continue, that inequalities are going to widen and that those on the wrong end of those trends will continue to be threatened.

Football is not going to have a change of heart. Though resistance is growing, the steamroller is going to keep on rolling unless the public, through the strength of their displeasure, force it to be stopped. Smaller clubs face an existence with no future. Larger clubs face a future with no soul. Whether that will happen, whether there is even a chance of it not happening, depends on questions wider than simply what is good for football.

The public, the wider community, is going to want to know why football clubs need to be kept in existence. Of what value are these football clubs? Football needs to justify itself, to show that if it disappears, then something real and irreplaceable is lost. If it can do so, if football makes a genuine contribution to the community, then it needs to be protected and preserved. You cannot simply step aside from anything that is of social worth, talk about harsh choices and economic realities and let it die.

Football matters. Of course its importance is blown out of all proportion. Football clubs face the threat of closure accompanied by nationwide press coverage, with fully-grown adults weeping in the streets. At the same time hospitals close without a murmur and with little more opposition than a few ignored petitions. Factories close, councils make redundancies, the unemployed are left to rot at home and nobody makes a fuss. The ugliness of inequality, the humiliation of poverty, both seem forgotten next to the avalanche of publicity for football.

Yet football matters and it matters for the same reasons as everything else. The struggle in football between the needs of profit and the needs of people is the same struggle which determines whether health shall be provided or whether it has to be paid for, whether people shall be helped or whether they shall struggle on their own, whether the owners of property shall be allowed to do as they please with their property or whether the rest of us are entitled to any consideration. The issues, albeit on a smaller scale, are the same.

We ought to keep it in perspective. The loss of football clubs is not to be measured against the loss of jobs and incomes. The loss of a football club may leave a gap in people's lives that nothing else can fill, but it is not the cause of suicide, of crime, of violence in the family and outside it. We ought to keep it in perspective but we never do. Football does not lend itself to keeping your perspective. But if we cannot keep football in perspective, let the perspective that prevails be ours, the perspective of supporters and of ordinary people, not the perspective of those whose understanding of the game runs no deeper than the contribution it makes to their growing fortunes.

Our football is a football of real value. It is not there solely as a means to make money, a parade of Premiership stars put to a hundred different commercial uses. Like anything else, its true value, its only value, is its value to society. But this value is more often commented on than understood. The word *community* is invoked without thinking what it really means, and football's contribution to the community is invoked without an understanding of what that contribution really is.

It is often claimed that when a football side does well, it improves productivity in local factories on a Monday morning, or when a national side does well, the nation puts in extra effort at work. We are invited to see this as a good idea. The prospect of doing more work for the same pay is proposed as a cause for celebration. If that is football's sole contribution to the community, we would be better off without it.

If football is there to paper over the cracks, to provide circuses where there is insufficient bread, then it would be of no use to us. That people watch football to take their minds off their problems is true enough, though it is no more true of football than of many other things. But if it were there deliberately for that reason, if it succeeded in that purpose, if Barnsley's promotion to the Premiership provided any more than the slightest distraction from the destruction wrought by closing down the pits, then that would be no service to the community. If football were the opium of the people, that is not something of which we should be proud. It is supposed to make a contribution to the community, not dull our senses while that community is beaten down and trampled on.

But what is that contribution? What is the relationship of a football club to the community? Football clubs may be named after the towns from which they spring but they do not *represent* them. The larger they are, the less they have anything to do with the immediate locality, while even the smaller clubs, in truth, represent nothing except themselves. It isn't even clear what community there is for them to represent. The term requires considerable qualification. Given the vast differences of living standards that prevail even in the smallest towns, to speak of a community is to invoke an ideal rather than the reality.

Of course there are times, when a smaller club fights through to an advanced stage of the FA Cup, when their colours are draped over the whole town and they dominate its conversation, when a temporary unity, a common purpose, is exerted by the local football club. But the unity is impermanent and unreal. After the crucial match, the inequalities remain. The well-off return to their well-off areas, the less well-off to theirs. The community is just as disunited, as segregated by income, as it ever was. Football does nothing to change that situation and therefore does nothing to alleviate it.

Most of the community in football is illusory. Much of the good it does is trivial, or is, in fact, no good at all. But for all its faults, football is valuable and totally irreplaceable. Its contribution is not just to the lives of fans as individuals, but to the quality of life which people living urban lives have the opportunity to enjoy.

Football clubs *represent* very little. Oxford is a particularly good example. I support Oxford United for no other reason than the fact that I have lived in Oxford, on and off, since 1983, including three appalling years at university and nearly a dozen better years since, living and working in the city. Those experiences were not two sides of a united whole. Oxford is less united, less of a community than any other town I know. In its way, it is almost as segregated as a Chicago suburb. The city and the university are separate and unequal, mutually suspicious, meeting up only on the basis of the one performing menial low-paid employment for the other.

The football club is the subject of some interest in one half of the city but inspires almost no interest whatsoever in the other. Oxford United is a most inappropriate term for the most disunited of cities. And what does Oxford United represent? When people think of Oxford, the place they think of is nothing to do with the football club. Think of Oxford and you think of what Oxford is not. You think of institutions which deliberately cut themselves off from Oxford. Oxford, to the outsider, is a tourist's city. United are rarely on their itinerary. In some cities a football club, the Liverpool of Shankly or the Napoli of Maradona, might be a way of drawing attention to the city, providing it with a symbol of its pride, something known and recognised across international borders. Rarely is this true of Oxford.

United don't even represent some sort of real Oxford, working Oxford, an Oxford east of the dividing line between the city and the colleges. United is not that powerful a symbol. It does not mobilise any great public feeling. It doesn't really represent us in that sense. It is not the repository of our civic pride. There are too many Manchester United shirts in Oxford, too many Chelsea stickers in the backs of cars, and too many people for whom football is not something of interest. United do not take up that much room in Oxford's mental landscape.

Go to Newcastle and the Toon are considered vital to the interests of that city, vital to its perception of its regional pride. More than that, you'll find many people who have never been to St James's Park, who do not even like football, but who can name all four sides of the ground. Everybody knows who manages the football club. Everyone can name the players. In Oxford, visiting supporters sometimes find it hard to get directions to the ground. United are not prominent. They are not representative. They are not considered crucial to the lives of very many of Oxford's citizens. Yet even in that relative obscurity, the football club is vital. We need it. Without it, the little element of community that remains in Oxford life would be whittled down to almost nothing.

Football is something that we do together. Watching football on your own is a thoroughly dissatisfying, incomplete experience. Football is about watching with other people. Football is a game created by the crowd. Its sense of togetherness, however limited and temporary, constitutes much of its appeal. The crowd is football. Football is not to be watched alone. In Oxford, football is something we do together *as Oxford*. There is precious little else that brings thousands together, in Oxford, for any common purpose.

There is the car factory at Cowley but even that has declined from the days when it employed more than 20,000 workers. The sense of community, engendered by the factory, or through the union, cannot be anything compared to what it was. There is quite a lot of music and entertainment in Oxford and sometimes this brings the city together physically. Every year there is a series of mini-carnivals in different parks across the city, of which the best and largest is on May Day. Oxford, in large numbers, meets together and appreciates each other's company. It is a better thing than the football club, more friendly, more relaxed, more communicative, more multiracial. But there is not enough of it. Oxford United play at home two dozen times a year and provide us with some sort of collective life. It isn't all that much. It addresses no social evils. It produces no lasting happiness. But it is real and important all the same.

One of the pleasures of living in a small city, for a number of years, is that you feel part of it. Almost every time you're out you see people you know and recognise, close friends whom you talk to, familiar faces with whom you exchange signs of recognition. Many of these familiar faces are people that you know from football. So the state of the local club becomes a common theme of conversation, a preoccupation. It is understood to be a vital aspect of our civic life. The people who consider it important are often the same individuals who take seriously the preservation of decent pubs, historic buildings, the provision of cinemas, the lamentable state of the local press and television. The reasons are the same. The discussions overlap.

We do take football seriously, and rightly so. There may not be much left by way of community but of what there is of it, football remains a part. In itself, it provides some of that community, provides an opportunity to be with other people. Football is a limited means of social communication. There is little you can do to speak and listen while you're in a football crowd. But there is more to football than the game. There is the pub, the friends, the shared interest, the conversation and the company, and these are better than most of what our modern, very private lives can offer us. You cannot meet people staying at home, watching the television, going out only in the car, or only with the family, or only when you go shopping. Football, at least, gets you out. It is a social activity.

You cannot make any sense of that if all you do is watch your football, on your own, on television. Such a narrow, such a limited vision of what football is about should not be allowed to outweigh the human value of the game. We live too much like that, alone, asocial, through the television. We live without variety. Instead of going to the cinema we rent a video. We get a carry-out instead of going up the pub.

We are invited to find our satisfaction on the Internet, to communicate with other people, not in person but through a screen. For all the genuine uses of the Internet, that is no way for human beings to relate with one another. As it becomes more possible for more of us to work from home, the awful vista presents itself of people working and shopping, even socialising, on their own, at home. When rich Americans can live in gated communities, designed to shut out undesirables, the spectre appears of all of us living that way in the future, as if we were living on the moon in private geodesic domes.

Even now, when we do go out, so much is false, similar, without character, as shops give way to hypermarkets and to shopping malls, as pubs turn into theme pubs, as more of life is spent on motorways. Against that background, football is a precious experience. It is real, and honest, and there is nothing fake about it. Not least because it always, almost always, lets us down.

Football is not the opium of the people. Sometimes it buys rich men a popularity they do not deserve but it never entirely buys our acquiescence and it never buys our silence. If it is intended as a form of social control then it does not do that job well. How would it help society if football clubs began to disappear? Losing our clubs would provide no hospitals, no schools, no jobs. Football does little harm in return for the pleasure and the human company it provides. It ought to be encouraged. The more there is of it, the better. There is no substitute for it. Watching the best teams in the world, on television, would not compensate Oxford supporters for the experience of watching even the worst teams they have ever seen.

United have nearly been lost to us more than once. Before Robert Maxwell took over, and in the aftermath of his death, and almost permanently afterwards, they have seemed uncertain to survive. They are anything but unique. Football clubs that used to exist hand-to-mouth, are now forced to get by on even less. Do we want towns and cities to provide the opportunity for their citizens to watch professional football, or do we want them to become duller places, emptier places, places with a smaller sense of worth?

That is football's value to the community. Football is valuable because community is valuable. Football matters because it matters how we live and how we want to live. It matters whether we are satisfied with an existence in which there is provided only what the market will provide, in which everything else is permitted to disintegrate. I do not want people, for those reasons, forced into living on the streets. Nor do I want to be deprived of my football club because of forces and decisions far beyond my control. The creation of poverty is more important than the game of football. But both matter. Both are related to the health of the community. That is reason enough why our football clubs must be preserved.

22. A COMMON TREASURY

The bandwagon is out of control. It has got to be stopped. But who is going to stop it for us? Who will act to restrain the powerful? Who will act to preserve clubs and to protect supporters? It is easy enough to come up with solutions. There are any number of ways in which the rules of football could be changed. There are any number of ways in which the authorities could intervene to restore the game to its previous balance, to prevent the abuse of power, to drag us back from the abyss. It is far harder to see how, in practice, these are going to happen. Far harder finding anyone who will take the action that we need. You can vote for whatever party you prefer, but if that party will not do the things you ask of it, who do you turn to then?

Yet if nobody will do these things, it doesn't follow that they can't be done. We are living at a time when it is considered wise to restrain expectations, to assume the market knows best and to accept that if what we have got is not enough, it is, nevertheless, the most we can expect. History is at an end. Alternatives are at an end. The intervention of governments in the economy is at an end. If this is true, then football, real football, is more than likely at an end as well.

But what passes for wisdom is merely pusillanimity. There is much that could be done by anyone with the power and the will to do it. Certainly it would require standing up to the most powerful forces in the game, and without doubt, the longer it is left, the more powerful those forces become, the harder the job of restraining them will be. But they are not all-powerful. They think they can make the rules but they are not exempt from having to follow them. And rules that have been

170

changed for the wrong reasons can be changed back for the right ones.

Admittedly, nobody within the structure of the game is going to act to reverse the changes which have endangered it. The Football League is a busted flush. It was comprehensively outmanoeuvred by the Football Association in the formation of the Premier League and since then it has presided over nothing but its own disintegrating body. The Football Association thought it was being very clever when it launched the *Blueprint*. But unfortunately it was creating Frankenstein's monster and now it cringes before its own creation. Power derives not from the Football Association but from the offices of the Premiership.

Even individual clubs, in open combat, are stronger than the Football Association. It must have known its number was up when, after it punished Tottenham for financial irregularities, Alan Sugar was able to go to court and have the punishment overturned. From that moment, even if the FA were not reduced to a shambling presence on the sidelines, the days of the self-contained world of football were still numbered. When Jean-Marc Bosman overthrew the transfer system in the European courts, the last rites were intoned. Decisions in the Dutch courts about the validity of television contracts have more bearing on the future of English football than anything that emanates from Lancaster Gate.

The rulings of judges override the rulings (assuming they still make any) of the football authorities. But laws interpreted in courts can be made, and changed, by governments. Football's fate will be decided in the political arena. Whether those with political power neglect and ignore it, or whether they defend it, will determine how much of the game survives. We need football to be defended. We therefore need the government to intervene as much as possible. Whether it be fashionable or not, we need a healthy dose of state interference in our affairs.

How do we need the state to interfere? Firstly, by subsidising football. There is no reason why smaller clubs cannot be supported from revenues other than their own. The same principle operates successfully in the arts, where subsidies of one sort or another keep many artistic institutions in existence. If public money can be used to subsidise opera, can it not be used to support the opera of the people?

It would be wrong, and crass, to counterpose the two, to demand that money be taken off one in order to support the other. That sort of suggestion is the province of the worst sort of Conservative MP, the kind whose real attitude to football could be gauged from their enthusiasm for ID cards. Football is not in competition with the arts. It is quite possible to enjoy both. Many thousands do. I would not want to take a penny from the National Gallery or Covent Garden. But why should we not be eligible for the same subsidy? Expensive seats at the Royal Opera House receive a subsidy that applied to a seat at Oxford United would enable me to watch the match for free. Why should football be entitled to nothing?

Football is not art. It does not debate, does not explain, does not enlighten, does not examine the nature of humanity. It cannot speak to people down the generations in the way that *King Lear* or *Madame Butterfly* can. But nevertheless it does speak to us, and its cultural value, let alone its social value, is not negligible. If it deserves to exist, then it deserves some subsidy too.

The money can be found. If necessary, sufficient funds can surely be located somewhere in the mountain of money created by the Lottery. I would much rather find it from the revenues of taxation. Every Saturday the Lottery makes me want to leave the country. Like the Premiership it seems, so soon after its creation, to be utterly impregnable, as if we couldn't do without it. Preying on the weakness and desperation of humanity, taking our money while harping on about its generosity, taking more from the poor than it does from the rich, it typifies everything that is sick and desperate about society.

It would be preferable to tax the rich. If windfall taxes on privatised utilities are acceptable, it should also be acceptable to levy a tax on the profits of the wealthiest football clubs. The situations are not quite identical. The utilities are in a position to exploit a natural monopoly and therefore to write their own pay cheques, a situation they have certainly abused. In contrast, football clubs are nominally in competition. Yet the differences are not that obvious. The bedrock support of the élite clubs, and their huge financial advantage, does give them, if not a natural monopoly, then something like it. They have certainly written their own pay cheques. If, as with the water and the rail companies, money is going to shareholders rather than being reinvested in players and supporters, then it would be better used for the interests of football.

Let us take a slice out of the Premiership's excessive profits. There is plenty to spare. They already give some conscience money to the Football Trust, £20 million over four years. It is a trifling sum compared to the money they get from television (£670 million) and if they are prepared to give it up for nothing, a little governmental muscle ought to produce a great deal more.

It ought to happen, but it probably won't. We will probably be left with the Lottery. We may as well fund football from the profits of the heroin trade as take anything from the Lottery. It is a tainted source if ever there was one. But beggars can't be choosers.

The original Lottery guidelines state that only capital projects can be assisted. But those rules can be changed. There is no reason why money can't be given to football clubs wholesale, like television money. Or, if we prefer, allocated by a panel of the great and good, like the Football Trust, according to whatever needs they perceive at individual clubs.

It will be objected that this will simply be a subsidy for lazy and inefficient directors, merely enabling them to foul up their clubs' finances even more. But it can always be made a condition of assistance that boards resign before assistance can be granted. It would be even better if directors had to possess qualifications, pass boards of inspection, obtain licences and regularly prove themselves fit to run clubs. There is no reason why clubs need to be run inefficiently. What makes them run inefficiently is the way in which any Tom, Dick or Harry with a few quid can get on the board, invite their mates to join them and then waste the club's money as they see fit. The occasional request from Companies House for the filing of accounts – most clubs ignore these requests and file late accounts as a matter of course – is not enough to keep these people in line. We need a strict regime of regulation.

If the government should regulate the directors of football clubs, they should also be prepared to regulate the game in general, more firmly than has ever been done before. It has been obvious, for years, that the old amateur arrangements by which football was run would never last long in the era of sport as big business. The outcome of that unequal struggle was that business, rather than football, began to determine the rules. Business is more powerful than football. But government ought to be more powerful still.

Football clubs should be protected by government regulation, protected from closure, just as the government prevents the wanton demolition of ancient buildings, of sites of special scientific interest, of the Green Belt. Clubs should be prevented from relocating unless the relocation is to another local site. Governments already have, and use, the power to prevent company takeovers when they are not in the public interest. Takeovers and feeder status can be forbidden.

Since we have a Government that looks to America for its social policy, they may as well look at what America does with sport. The greatest of caution should be exercised. American sport is about forming cartels, not about preventing them. It is about maximising profit, not about maximising public access, and certainly not about restricting ticket prices. Yet it does have one central principle to recommend it. It insists that clubs are not commercially independent of their leagues. They cannot sign whatever deals they choose. They cannot even freely sign the players that they want. The interests of the sport come first.

In the interests of football, action needs to be taken to reduce the commercial advantage of the largest clubs. Nobody wants a totally level playing field. The idea is that clubs should be of varying size, should enjoy different prospects and perspectives. But they should not wipe each other out economically. Compensation should be paid for players in such a way that the Bosman judgement does no harm.

Restrictions should be placed on the number of professional players that any one club is able to employ at any time. Such an edict, by itself, would undo much of the damage done by the growing income gap. You can have as much money as you want, but if you can't buy all the players that you want, then smaller clubs will still be able to keep them. They will not all be playing for the reserves or doing nothing just so long as they aren't playing for anybody else.

It is a ludicrous situation, another rip-off of the fans. It is as if the National Gallery were to make expensive acquisitions and then lock them, unseen, in the basement, purely so that the Louvre couldn't have them instead. Premiership sides employ 40 or more professionals. We pay for these players. But we never get to see them. A stop should be put to this. Restrict clubs to a given number of professionals, say 30, and permit them to use no more than two dozen in any given season. I imagine the élite clubs would howl and wail about any such restriction, claiming it took away their right to employ anyone they chose. But squad limits exist in other sports. Even if they failed against a legal challenge, the law can be changed. It would be in the supporters' interest. We would get to see the players we pay for. We would enjoy a more even game. It might not be in the interests of John Hall and his friends. But we can probably live with that.

How is this to happen? There is no tradition of government regulation of the day-to-day business of football but in itself that is no reason why it shouldn't happen. Football clubs are already regulated by the state. Before any club can play football, it is obliged to obey and implement the requirements of the Football Licensing Authority whose regulations relate to stadium safety. In principle, such an authority ought to be able to rule on any aspect of football that it pleased. All sorts of regulations in respect of other industries are enacted to ensure free and fair competition, to prevent monopoly. Football needs as much regulation of that sort as can be enacted.

The government has the power to create a body with overall power in football, able to override the Premiership if it sees fit to do so. Such a body should be created and should see fit to do so. Its purpose need not be restricted to looking after the economic well-being of the game. There are so many things that it could do. As football shows no sign of addressing the exclusion of black people from its stands, as its response consists of little more than warm words and the occasional statement in the programme, then such a body could insist that football clubs implement determined programmes to increase the proportion of their support that comes from ethnic minorities, that they be obliged to demonstrate their progress and should face penalties if they do not show results. It is time to make these people jump a bit.

They can be made to jump, and to knuckle under. If the Government established a ruling body for football, independent of the Halls and the Deins, that body could proceed to make whatever rules it felt like. It could restructure the game according to what is best for everyone. For instance, if inequality of income is not to render competition so one-sided as to be meaningless, then different parts of the game cannot be allowed to negotiate separate television deals. The money needs to be used for the benefit of all football clubs, not just those who have too much already. No separate Premiership should exist. The top division should be no more than that. The summit, the apex, but not the dictator.

Still less can individual clubs be allowed to sign their own television deals. There is no reason why they should expect to be allowed to. They do not set up their own games and play them independently of anybody else. They are members of leagues, they play in cup competitions with other clubs. Football clubs do not exist independently of each other. Yet they want it both ways. If they want to sell their own television rights then they should be invited to go and play on their own.

Governments have the power to pass laws to make companies of any sort, including football clubs, obey the social good as well as their own good. It will be objected that European legislation makes it impossible for Westminster to make its own rules. In particular it may not have the power to decide that football clubs do not have the right to sign whatever contracts they see fit. But all that means is that the problem is a European one. The Dutch judgement which wrecked their country's arrangements for televised football has only succeeded in putting still more power in the hands of Ajax, Feyenoord and PSV. In Italy, Juventus, Inter and Milan have 60 per cent of the pay-per-view income between them. In Spain, in France, in Sweden and in Germany, the same pattern is certain to emerge. Football is at risk in much the same way everywhere. Who cares whether the response comes from Westminster or Brussels? But a response, of some sort, there must be.

I do not expect such a response to come. What is proposed above seems very radical. But it only seems so because we are accustomed to the unwillingness of governments to act against the power of the market. In fact, nothing proposed here is radical at all. There is almost nothing here for which an equivalent does not exist in one part or another of our cultural or commercial life. Restrictions on the independence of businesses are not unheard of. Cultural interests are not assumed to be totally subject to the interests of commerce. The subsidy of all sorts of bodies and institutions continues to exist. It ought to be easy for the Government to say that football is important, it needs to be looked after, and to legislate to ensure that this happens. But this is exactly what they do not have the political will to do.

Labour is a lot better for football supporters than the Conservatives. The Conservatives were the enemies of football supporters. We were among their favourite scapegoats. All John Major's photo-opportunities at Chelsea, all David Mellor's appearances on the radio masquerading as one of us, could not wipe out the memories of the ID-card scheme. That scheme quite certainly contributed to the defeat of the offensive Colin Moynihan in the 1992 election and it was among the many reasons to cheer the demolition of the whole bunch of them in 1997.

At the time that scheme was introduced, Labour was our ally, working with our representatives against the scheme, opposing it in Parliament. It is hard to be sure how they would react now. If an ID-card scheme had been suggested by Michael Howard in the dog days of the Tory Government, would Jack Straw have risked his law-and-order reputation by opposing it? But whatever happens, Labour will always be closer to supporters than the Conservatives. There has never been a Labour Minister (or Shadow Minister) for Sport who has been hostile to football fans. There has never been a Conservative Minister for Sport who has been our friend.

But being our friend is not enough. It will require state intervention, heavy state intervention, to protect football, and such intervention is not going to come from the sort of Labour Government which thinks that state intervention is no longer possible, or even desirable.

This Labour Government believes that what is good for business is good for the rest of us. Its leading members are anxious to be seen at every opportunity with leading representatives of business. It is unlikely to act against the leading representatives of business in football. In the 1997 election, Labour specifically sought out Alan Sugar's support. Tony Blair met with Rupert Murdoch and went out of his way to reassure him about Labour's intentions. This helped win him the

176

approval of the *Sun* and the *News Of The World*. But anything that can be done to look after football's interests would, necessarily, involve acting against the ability of the Sugars and the Murdochs to pursue their interests in whatever manner they may please. Labour will not do that any more. It does not believe either that it can or that it should.

The Government did set up something called a 'Task Force', something between an investigation committee and a discussion group, a body without statutory powers but one whose remit allowed it to investigate all aspects of contemporary football and identify the major problems. It is hard to know what to make of the Task Force, with its mixture of gimmick and goodwill, with the optimism caused by the inclusion of Adam Brown from the Football Supporters Association balanced by the pessimism induced by the invitation to Roland Smith, chairman of Manchester United. (In itself, the concept of including representatives from all parts of the game, while appearing reasonable, is actually absurd. Ultimately there is no common ground, no mutually acceptable philosophy, in a game that is pulling in different and opposite directions.) The choice, as its leader, of David Mellor, a member of the most vile government this country has had this century, is too silly and too sickly to bear thinking about.

Yet it is good that the Task Force exists, and good things will come out of it. But it is most likely that it will identify major problems and then prescribe minor palliatives, that it will address symptoms but not causes. This is less the fault of the Task Force than of the Government that appointed it. The philosophy of the present government is not to interfere when interference is exactly what we need, and its economics are those of the free market when that very free market is the problem.

The free market poses the real threat to football. That market depends on its ability to close down businesses which do not make a profit. Not only can it close them down, it has to be able to. Without that threat there is no pressure to cut costs, to fight for markets. The market *must* close down companies that, by its standards, fail. Let it loose in football, whose clubs do not tend to make a profit, whose clubs, by the nature of things, fail more often than they succeed, and those clubs cannot possibly survive.

It is the market which stretches the financial differentials in the game beyond all toleration, which enables clubs to charge whatever they fancy for tickets, which ensures that the financial clout of television prevails over the needs of supporters. It is a bull in football's china shop. But Labour, rather than preserve the china, admires the strength and dynamism of the bull. *The rigour of competition and the discipline of the market.* That is what they believe in now. If you believe in that, there is not very much you can do to solve the problems that bedevil football. Labour has the power, but it will not use it. Any measures it takes will fail to address the real scope of the problems. It is no good looking to the Labour Party for a lead.

Labour takes what is realistic and by rejecting intervention, makes it idealistic. Then let us be idealists. There is plenty of room for idealism the way football is run now. And football fans are usually idealists. If we were realists we would all have given up years ago. We expect the impossible of our clubs and we spend decades waiting to see it happen. We are not predisposed to be reasonable and we are by our very nature inclined to dream.

If we are to dream, we ought to dream of taking the ownership of our clubs out of private hands. Football clubs are run for personal profit, or for publicity, and even when owners do act in the club's interests, there is still no way for the supporters to formally exercise their influence. No way, either, to prevent the club being sold on to less satisfactory owners. We are told little and asked less.

Ownership is the problem. Any clown or crook can own a football club, and many do. Take ownership out of their hands and we would be freed from these people's incompetence, their secrecy, their ego, their scheming, their contempt for the supporters. Take ownership out of private hands in football generally and we might have an end of football for the purposes of private profit, and a return to football for the purposes of playing football.

Idealistic this may seem. But even this is not so very radical. County cricket clubs are run by their members. Smaller football clubs may very well turn to their supporters for help in the future, if only because they have nowhere else to go. The rescue of Bournemouth was achieved by creating a Trust which gave the supporters some degree of control over their club. There are elements of fans' control even at the highest levels. Barcelona is probably the richest, most free-spending club in the world, yet you cannot run the club, no matter how rich you may be, without standing for election by the *socios*, the members of Barcelona.

All sorts of organisations, even organisations which spend many millions, are owned by their members, and sometimes subject to their votes. Those building societies which have not yet abandoned mutuality remain the property of their members. There are many different ways in which common ownership exists, many different levels of accountability. But clearly, football clubs do not *have* to be a private fief.

They could be owned by their supporters. Or they could be owned by the community, through the offices of local councils. Clubs are not very large as companies go. Most local authorities already manage far bigger operations than a football club. A small club in the First Division may have a staff, including players, of less than 50 employees, a turnover of not much more than two million pounds a year. Compared to the average council workforce, that is very small beer indeed.

This is not at all the mainstream economic wisdom. It is nothing that our government will do, nothing that it will allow local authorities to do. It would not appeal to club owners who sell expensive tickets that local fans cannot afford. But it is possible. Football clubs in the hands of local people. Football clubs in the hands of their supporters. That is how it should be.

Football should not be the plaything of private individuals. Just as insecurity has swept through the workforce, so it has swept through the world of the football supporter, making what seemed permanent seem uncertain to survive. Football supporters have always observed that while managers and players and chairmen come and go, the supporters and their clubs always remain. If that truth is to be preserved, then one way or the other, the clubs and their supporters need to come together. They are our clubs. It is our game. Morally we own the game already. It should be, practically and permanently, ours.

23. THEM AND US

I'm proud to be a football supporter. I think I ought to be. It's not a stupid thing to feel. It's not a chauvinistic pride, a loyalty to flags, nor is it the sentimental pride that supporters often feel, in their colours or in the players that play for them. I understand that not much is achieved through football and I understand the limitations of the game. Yet I am still proud, and glad, to be a football supporter.

I like football supporters. There is nothing else I would prefer to do on a Saturday than be with other supporters, watching football, talking about football. I know we have our share of fools, and worse. I know there are too many supporters for whom football is an opportunity to be boorish, to be unpleasant, to make a lot of other people uncomfortable at the thought of sharing football grounds with them. But without forgetting for a moment all its faults and its deficiencies, I like the football crowd. I like its passion and I like its honesty.

Perhaps if I had not lived in Oxford, I might not appreciate it quite so much. But in a city stuffed with the smug and the pompous, with the sort of people who speak down to people, with the sort who are extremely pleased with themselves, it is a pleasure, a relief to be part of the football crowd. It does us good, I think. It gives us something. And it is something to be proud of.

I don't think that *proud* is overstating the case. For the 15 years that I have been going to football matches, supporters have been under attack. In recent seasons it has been an economic assault, with the game becoming more and more expensive. At the same time we have to put up with the complaints of owners of the major clubs, who demand more money, more opportunity to make more money, and refuse to accept that *we* have anything to complain about. The pressure, the feeling of power being exercised against supporters, is becoming intense.

But before that, before we became a financial opportunity for chairmen and shareholders, we were under attack as a public order problem and a scapegoat. If you are relatively new to football, you will know what it is like to be ripped off, but you may not know what it is like to be publicly despised. The fences have mostly disappeared now but it is impossible to forget the spikes, the barbed wire, the electric wire Ken Bates tried to put up at Chelsea. It was a time of being refused service in pubs, of the casual assumption that you were a hooligan, of the automatic association of football not with enjoyment but with death and violence. But we came through it. We come through it still. We refuse to give in or to go away. That is something to be proud about.

We get little enough respect for that commitment. That is how football works. Supporters show great loyalty to their clubs and get precious little in return. We are taken for granted. It is all right to take our money, the more the better. But when we expect something back we are too often fickle, out of line, disloyal, at best impatient. It is all right to take our money but not to accept its implications that we have expectations that we want to be fulfilled. Football is all about the loyalty of supporters and the many ways it is abused.

Loyalty is expected to include the fans refraining from criticism. We don't expect people to thank us for our criticisms, still less do we expect that they will like it when we call for them to go. Football is an insecure profession, if not for chairmen, then certainly for managers and players, and of course they are sensitive about their jobs and their reputations, quite apart from a natural unwillingness to be shouted at and criticised. And there is always the tendency of the professional to close ranks against the public, in the same way that the actor, or the musician, may consider the public to be ignorant and uninformed. From the perspective of the professional, they are the game, the supporters are outside it, and we do not know what we are talking about.

But they treat criticism from the press in the same way, which makes it doubly remarkable how little the media accept that we have the right to call for people's heads, that managers, players and chairmen have to live up to our expectations. It is common to see supporters criticised for wanting the manager out, but it is rare to see, in print, anybody agree with them. The assumption is that we demand too much and that we should put up with what we get. Sometimes you would think that we weren't part of the game at all, that we were just outsiders looking in, outsiders whose comments are out of order and are not required.

When Leeds supporters grew tired of Howard Wilkinson and brought about a change of management at Elland Road, their reward for their trouble was to be described, in the *Guardian,* as 'yobs and bigots'. Yobs and bigots. Described in terms more appropriate to thugs and racists, just because they wanted a new manager. That is an extreme example but it is an attitude more common than sympathy with the supporters. When Aberdeen fans wanted Roy Aitken sacked, I heard Roddy Forsyth, on the radio, comment that 'we don't like to hear that sort of thing at football matches'. To the supporter that was the most curious of comments. What did he mean by *we*? There can be few supporters who have never called for a manager to go. We don't just like to hear that sort of thing, we do that sort of thing whenever we think it necessary. So who are this *we* to whom this is not acceptable behaviour? Clearly it is a *we* which does not encompass the supporters.

You would think that the game existed without us, took place of its own accord. We pay for football. If for no other reason, we have the right to say what we please because it is our money making everything go round. And the more money we pay, the more right we surely have. If it was not acceptable to call for managers to be sacked when football cost three pounds a head to watch, is it not a bit more understandable when it costs £20? But the money is not really what this is about. It is about our expectations and what football would be without them.

Everybody wants us to care. They want a crowd. They want it for the money, they want it for the spectacle, they want it for the atmosphere, they want it for the support it gives the team. They want us to make football a cockpit of emotion. They want us to put our heart and soul into supporting our club. That is what we do. The game would be nothing, would move nobody, were it not for the support of the football crowd, and that support would be nothing without our expectations.

We desire. Because we desire, we demand. We are prepared to shout ourselves hoarse when it is called for and by the same token, for the very same reasons, we are prepared to shout with discontent when that is called for. They want the one but not the other. They want our desperation for our team to win, but then they don't want our desperation for our team to win. That is not the disloyalty of supporters. It is the disloyalty of football towards the supporters.

If we must weigh it up in economic terms, why do managers imagine they are paid what they are if not because they are expected to produce results? Football is a very well-paid profession, yet those who are well paid complain that too much is being asked of them. Possibly they are right. Too much is being asked of them. But they are only so well paid because too much is being asked of them. We all expect our teams to win, which is impossible. Our expectations are unrealistic, but as a consequence the salaries on offer are equally unrealistic. Football wants the one but not the other. It wants our contribution but it does not want to be called upon to satisfy our requirements in return.

The more money comes into it, the less they expect to be answerable to people who provide it. Many people make so much money out of football now that they find it intolerable to be called to account by the mere public. Like the fat cats of the utilities, they believe that reward is their own justification. If they are paid hundreds of thousands they must be worth it, otherwise nobody would be paying them that money. And if they are worth hundreds of thousands, why should they waste time on the opinions of people who are not worth one tenth, or one twentieth of that amount? It is rare to find a manager who will treat the opinions of supporters with respect. Few are prepared to put themselves in supporters' shoes. Among prominent managers in recent years, perhaps only Kevin Keegan has done credit to his profession, prepared as he was, on the day he sold Andy Cole, to spend hours explaining himself to the supporters face to face. That gesture stood out precisely because of its singularity. There is a distance between managers and supporters which is unbridgeable and which is going to get wider.

There is a distance between football and its supporters which is also getting wider and which we struggle, seemingly in vain, to close. In many ways my time as a supporter, the last decade and a half, has been a terribly discouraging time to be a football fan. It has been one thing after another, each blow to football succeeded by another. All the increased popularity of football cannot obscure how difficult that time has been. But at the same time as it has been discouraging, it has been encouraging and exciting too, as supporters have fought back, have stood up for their opinions and their interests. Football has marginalised the supporters. But the supporters have responded.

While football has got worse, we have got better. We have not just learned to fight back on our account, but we have begun to learn to co-operate with each other. We can trace this back at least as far as the response to Thatcher's ID-card scheme, when petitions were collected at most grounds in the country, and in the formation at much the same time of the Football Supporters' Association. Magazines like *When Saturday Comes* and *The Absolute Game* assumed a worldview in which supporters needed to know what other supporters at other clubs were thinking. In Scotland, supporters of many different clubs were involved in the Hands Off Hibs campaign, seeing, in Wallace Mercer's ambition, a contempt for supporters they recognised and felt they needed to oppose.

These phenomena may have been small in numbers. Insignificant compared to the vast numbers of supporters who did not join campaigns and organisations of this sort. But they were reflected by a wider sympathy among supporters for the supporters of other clubs. It is intangible, passive, fleeting. Often it is expressed in no manner more material than the supporters of one team joining in the other's chants against the board. And sometimes the intention is only to mock. But more often it is a statement of sympathy and a sign that supporters are more aware than before of what is going on elsewhere in football, and much more aware that what is going on affects them.

Many supporters are more than aware, are positively alarmed about the future of the game, are made extremely nervous by some of the things that have been going on. They feel that it is time a line was drawn, that it is up to fans to draw it, and that we cannot wait until our own particular club is threatened before we draw that line. This was most visibly expressed in the campaign to save Brighton and Hove Albion from extinction at the hands of its own board.

What appalled supporters was not that Brighton had been relegated to the Third Division, which had happened to many other clubs before them, nor even that they risked demotion to the Conference, which fate has befallen several other clubs. These were alarming symptoms of decline, but they were not what the fans found shocking. What shocked supporters was that Brighton were on the brink of closure and that they were in the position because of the actions of an absentee chairman, who was closing their ground, but who was still making a lot of money out of this threatened club. Yet his investment in that club amounted to the sum of £56.25.

Bill Archer, who lived in Lancashire and worked in Crewe, bought out his fellow Brighton directors for less than sixty quid by telling them that if he did not take sole control, Albion would go bankrupt, leaving considerable debts for which they would then be responsible. The other directors leapt for safety. But Archer appeared to be neither confident about saving the club nor concerned whether it was saved or not. He was, however, concerned about what the club could do for him.

Until Archer took over the constitution of the club had stated, wisely, that no director of the club could benefit from its closure. If it closed, anything left over was to be distributed to other local sports clubs.

Therefore no director could envisage closing down the club for their own profit. Archer, in sole control and therefore able to alter the constitution, had the clause removed. He could therefore make money if the ground were sold. It then became apparent that the ground had, indeed, been sold.

While this was going on, the chairman's loan of £600,000 which was propping up the club, and which had previously appeared in the accounts as interest-free, appeared in subsequent accounts as eligible for interest. This amounted to around £350,000. There was a penalty clause attached by which if the club, controlled by Archer, failed to make the interest payments on time, they would owe Archer a further quarter of a million. The payments were not made. The debt to Archer increased.

The club was paying out most of its money to its own chairman. It had sold its ground but had not found another one. The chairman was never at the ground. At this point Brighton fans began to panic. Their patience snapped. The last home game of the 1995-96 season, which fans had been told would be the last one at the Goldstone, saw the pitch invaded and the game abandoned.

A lot of abuse was piled upon them for this. ITN news described events as the return of hooliganism, distorting the truth for the purposes of sensationalism. The events, like all riots, were blamed on outsiders, as if that could explain them. Some supporters thought that the pitch invasion didn't help. But it had the one great virtue of bringing the developments in Brighton into the public eye, of making clear to everyone the strength of feeling among supporters and of convincing other supporters that something had to be done.

When other supporters heard what was happening in Brighton they were appalled. But they were well aware that it could happen somewhere else. The Goldstone was not the first ground to be sold without a new ground being located first. Brighton were not the first club to risk closure because of neglect in the boardroom. Bill Archer was not the first chairman to do well for himself out of an otherwise failing football club. Brighton supporters were not the first to find the fate of their club decided behind closed doors. Brighton was the worst combination of all these that anyone had heard of. But the most important thing was that at the same time it was typical.

What wasn't typical, what was unique, was the reaction of other supporters. The following season events dragged on, but no progress towards a new ground, or towards the club's survival, appeared to be made. The chairman's house in Blackburn was picketed by supporters.

The club were allowed one more year at the Goldstone provided they paid the new landowners £20,000 a week. Leaders of the protests were barred from the ground. Time was getting short. So other supporters at other clubs determined to take sides and break the impasse.

A teenage Plymouth fan suggested that the only way to mobilise outside support was to hold a demonstration at the Goldstone. And on a Saturday in February that is what happened. Thousands of supporters, from dozens of different clubs, descended on Brighton to protest at Bill Archer and to protest at the failure of the Football Association to do anything to stop him. There were supporters from Scotland, from Spain and Germany, and there were messages of support from every continent.

I am proud to be a football supporter. I was proud to be one that day. It was an extraordinary sight, thousands of supporters meeting in a park and gathering outside the ground, and then the shirts and scarves of dozens of different clubs packed on to the same terrace. This had never happened in England before, not in all the hundred years and more of professional football. Thousands of us, used, by the very nature of football, to supporting our club and opposing everybody else's. But on that day we demanded nothing for ourselves. We just refused to see our fellow supporters treated so contemptibly.

For every supporter who was present, there must have been dozens of sympathisers, watching their own club, but following events all the same. And no one who went is likely to forget the sight, or sound, of these supporters chanting *football, united, will never be defeated*, not *supporters* but *football*, because the one and the other are the same.

What good did it do? Did we win? We can't know exactly how much influence we had on subsequent events, whether we built up the pressure to a point where it became intolerable. But the club did not die. The Albion were taken over, and although Archer remained on the board, he was obliged to issue a statement apologising for his actions.

The situation was complicated by Brighton's fight to avoid relegation to the Conference. Supporters of Hartlepool and Hereford may have felt aggrieved. But it was the right thing, an important thing, for us to have done because of what it achieved for Brighton, because of what it achieved for us. It was probably the most important event in football that season, far more important than cup finals and European matches. It may have been a turning point for football, for its supporters. It may have been the moment that we learned that solidarity is necessary and that solidarity can win.

Yet there is something strange about that information. We shouldn't want to know it. *Opposition, organisation, solidarity*: these are political words, words which are about hard work and sacrifice and spending time supporting good causes against unfavourable odds. These are not the reasons why we are attracted to football. If we wanted to devote our time to political involvement, there are plenty of ways of doing so. It might be a more constructive and more socially useful thing to do. But we want to watch football instead.

It is a refuge from politics. For my part, while I have always been interested in football, I found it all the more comfortable, all the more attractive, as a way to avoid political involvement. Once the left had been crushed in the Eighties, crushed in the miners' strike, crushed in the Labour Party, crushed internationally, not all of us fancied another decade or so fighting losing battles, and we dropped away. When the poll tax was demolished by the giant demonstration in Trafalgar Square, I was watching Oxford at Oakwell. I didn't regret it. Football was less tiring, less wearing, less depressing. Even when fanzines came along, I didn't feel I was doing any more than having my say about a game I loved. Most people involved in fanzines would likely say the same. Football isn't politics. It is something very different. It's just that it doesn't seem to be as different as it used to be.

It cannot be that different when football clubs are floated on the stock market, when clubs are judged in terms of their profitability, when chairmen are making millions. It doesn't look that different when everybody notices, everybody talks about, the gap between the richest and the poorest, when football is about the courts and the politicians.

We wanted football to be a different world entirely. We wanted it to be separate from the real world. It never was, entirely, but you could pretend it was. For many decades it was separate enough. It seemed all the more separate because it seemed indestructible, because we could assume that what was there one year was still going to be there ten years hence. Now it isn't indestructible. It isn't separate. It isn't very different at all.

The role supporters play in football is not so very different from the role of working people in the wider world. They are expected to work as hard as possible, to show self-sacrifice and dedication, but if they demand a rise in their standard of living they are advised not to be greedy, to settle for what they have got. The employers, by contrast, are expected to try and make as much money as they can on the grounds that their avarice is the motor of the economy. *We* are enjoined to spend our money on our football clubs, to get behind them, to be the willing foot-soldiers. If we are dissatisfied by the results, we are expected not to show it. But while we pay for football, monetarily and otherwise, the chairmen expect to be financially rewarded for their time, and at the same time be praised for showing generosity.

So football, like the society that breeds it, divides into them and us. They do very well indeed out of us and they are in no way grateful for it. And the better that they do, the more power they have, the less we seem able to do about it. They tower over us. They dominate us.

Yet, even at the apex of their success, they are nervous of us, unsettled by our discontent, afraid of our reactions. They are unwilling to let us get close to them. They can bear our money but not our company. Occasionally they come on the pitch for our applause, if everything is going well and they are guaranteed a good reception. But otherwise they are usually invisible to the fans. Bill Archer rarely went within 200 miles of Brighton, but he was only exceptional in that he avoided the ground as well as those who filled it.

There are exceptions. But most directors rarely mix with fans, save for their cronies and supporters, and the more important the director, the bigger the club, the more distant they are. They have their directors' box, their private lounge, their boardroom and their reserved place in the car park. They have these things because they do not wish to mix with us.

The more they make us pay for football, the more our expectations rise, but the more often those expensive expectations are disappointed. The football crowd is often an angry crowd and it knows where most of that anger ought to be directed. The more directors profit from the game, the more they are the subjects of our ire. Yet that anger is rarely anything more than harsh words thrown into empty space, a tide which, however intimidating it looks, inevitably dissipates itself. Our words may hurt but we are no more threatening to them than that.

But there is an enormous energy in a football crowd. There is nothing to match that crowd, that mass of people, row upon row, thousands wedded to a common cause. When moved, its voice is unforgettable, whether conveying triumph, anticipation or despair. It is a sound louder than any other human sound that I have ever heard, a sound of irresistible power.

If that crowd wanted, it could sweep everything before it. When it expresses that power, when you are in a great stadium, a packed ground, and the crowd, already in a frenzy, erupts at a goal, listen to that crowd. Watch that crowd and consider what could withstand that power. Nothing could. That, the power of the crowd, is what the directors are scared of. But it is far more powerful than that. That power, the movement of the mass, is the power which at other times, in other places, causes governments to shake.

That power is usually dormant, unused. Unknown, for the most part, even to itself. In the football crowd, more often than elsewhere, it finds its voice. The crowd gathers, flexes its muscles, acts in unison. But because football, when all is said and done, is no more than a small part of our lives, the crowd is not dangerous. Exploited as it is, patronised for its loyalty, insulted when it asks for something in return, it is a sleeping giant, and football is not cause enough for it to wake. But still, seeing these millions who watch football, those millions who by their efforts keep society going, who receive so little in return – who can perceive our power, the power of that crowd, and not think:

What could they do? What could they do about it? What could they do about it if we move?